The Full
Digital Nation

Violaine Champetier de Ribes
Jean Spiri

The Full
Digital Nation

Estonia:
A Break In The GAFAM Wall

Translated from french
by Nafkote Tamirat

10¹⁴

Cent Mille Milliards

First published in France 2018

Copyright © Violaine Champetier de Ribes, Jean Spiri
and Cent Mille Milliards, 2019

Introduction

Imagine a country where the State doesn't have the right to ask any citizen for the same information twice. Imagine a country where, with a single card, you can complete all administrative actions, with the exceptions of marriage, divorce and real estate purchases (and that's by choice and only for now.) Imagine a country where you can take out a loan and vote in mere minutes, and without leaving your home. Imagine a country where both the very young and the very old have been trained in digital technologies for over 20 years. Imagine a country where the State can adjust laws in less than six months at the request of start ups. Imagine a country where you can create a company in 18 minutes. Imagine a country conceiving the State as an inclusive services platform, whose main job is to simplify and improve the daily lives of its citizens. Imagine a country where internet access has been a fundamental right since 2000. Imagine a country where the digital transformation and transparency of the State, along with the trust it has established with its citizens, are reasons for pride and part of the nation's marketing campaign...

That country is Estonia. Its time as holder of the presidency of the Council of the European Union, from July to December 2017, brought to light a State model that digital experts had known about for years and which the general public began to discover. The "most advanced digital society in the world" according to *Wired* magazine (2017), Estonia also occupies one of the top spots in the PISA education rankings[1] and one of the highest rates of start ups per capita in the EU, with Skype spearheading the wave and four unicorns (companies valued at over one billion dollars) already. There is also a remarkably seamless relationship between the citizens of Estonia and their public administrations, especially considering how the country has over 1.3 million inhabitants, who speak a rather unknown language. What's more, since 2014, this digital identity and the services coming with it can be used by citizens across the globe through e-Residency, the transnational digital programme that gives access to an administrative and economic environment that's well-suited to today's breed of nomadic company creators.

This isn't just a matter of good practices, however: what Estonia is inventing is a model for a citizen-centric nation-state for the digital age. There's no doubt that Estonia is the world's first platform-State which is willing to go beyond its borders and respond to the very predictable crisis facing the concept of the nation-state at a time when GAFAM (Google, Apple, Facebook, Amazon, Microsoft) are inventing

---

1. PISA: Programme for International Student Assessment

a transnational solutionism[2]. This idea that in the near future, large digital companies will be the best-equipped to concretely address the needs of citizens should be pushing States to wonder what they will base their legitimacy on in that world of tomorrow. In this context, the example of Estonia can tell us a great deal about the future of France, as well as that of the European Union. It can also concretely respond to the idea that traditional States are growing obsolescent: in the next 10 years, and with the changes brought by today's civilisation, these States face the real risk of watching the "uberisation" of their legitimacy. Along with the digital era comes unprecedented change and sprawling developments from GAFAM, which finds itself in a position where it's able to provide the services that, up until now, were the exclusive prerogative of the State, thus contributing to the erosion of States' sovereignty.[3] In that respect, GAFAM has become their direct competitor, minus the values of public service or democratic arbitration. This move has been expedited by the inertia of many States in the face of platform development. In this sense, Estonia is an exception: is its model an antidote to GAFAM's hegemony? What is clear is that this country is establishing new global standards for digital and platform States, thereby introducing an alternative to the solutionist model coming out of Silicon Valley.

---

2. Solutionism: a term coined by Evgueni Morozov that refers to the ideology he believes to be inherent in GAFAM's actions, namely, that they bring solutions that seem politically-minded but in fact, lack the democracy that such solutions would require.

3. Gilles Babinet: "There is a shift in sovereignty from States to GAFA." *France Inter*; August 14, 2018.

While the country celebrated the centenary of its independence interspersed with 50 years of Soviet occupation—on February 24, 2018, we must take a look at the specifics of this achievement. This isn't to say that we should brush off this model as being too difficult to adapt in countries with larger populations and with States that have had longer histories. French Prime Minister Édouard Philippe, ex-French Secretary of State for Digital Affairs, Mounir Mahjoubi, and Minister of Public Action and Accounts, Gérald Darmanin, aren't wrong when they increasingly refer and travel to Estonia in their vision of the French State's digital transformation. At the European level, the Tallinn Declaration of September 2017 not only suggests advances that could be made toward a digital Europe, but also lays the foundations for reflection about digital sovereignty and a model that would be suitable for the European Union. As President of Estonia, Kersti Kaljulaid, puts it: "Compared to other countries in the world, Estonia is better prepared for the time we're living in: it's a homeland that's available on the internet and provides a point of reference for both citizens and e-residents."[4]

Our crush on Estonia

This is a book born from encounters: those of the authors with each other and with Estonia, as well as many other meetings with the people who lent their

---

4.   Extract from the brochure "Estonia Oh Surprise!", published by the Estonian Ministry of Foreign Affairs.

testimonies to this book. It comes from a desire to understand the ins and outs of this Estonian model, to go further than postcards and to never forget that this model is the result of a culture and a state of mind.

Violaine Champetier de Ribes relates, "I discovered Estonia in May 2017 during a trip that was organized by Jean-Michel Billaut, a pioneering and passionate explorer of new technologies and president and founder of l'Atelier BNP Paribas[5]. I wanted to see what a totally digitised country looked like, but I had no clear idea of what we were going to discover. It was the political project at the heart of the digital State that struck me: this was a country truly at the service of citizens and entrepreneurs. Citizens are considered clients, whom the State can best serve by simplifying their lives. I'm convinced that therein lies the key to the success of this new model of the State in the digital era: by placing the citizen at the centre of public activities, the success of any public digital programme led by the State is guaranteed.

I'd like to point out that Jean-Michel Billaut deserves a great deal of credit, as he is 72 years old and disabled, with an amputated leg due to a medical error. Our group leader rattled about on the cobblestones of old Tallinn in a wheelchair, launching himself into this exploration of Estonia. His limitless curiosity compelled him to stop every single Estonian whose path we crossed in order to ask about their internet bandwidth at home. Their response was always the same: "I have no idea. All I know is, it works." During

---

5.   An innovation lab of the French bank.

our week there, whenever we were leaving a place, Jean-Michel rewarded us with a booming, "We are so SCREWED!" At the end of one presentation on the e-Ambulance programme (see Chapter 4), he got emotional, remarking: "If we had had this solution in France, I wouldn't have lost my leg."

Billaut notes: "I had found my way to Estonia quite naturally. I became an e-Resident to see what it had to offer. It was a matter of opportunity, because I met the Estonian ambassador to Paris, His Excellency Alar Streimann[6]. I asked him to help me go see it for myself and I ended up going with friends. I went expecting to understand how a nation, which just 25 years ago had been crushed by Soviet rule and its oppressive bureaucracy, was able to become the first fully digital nation in the world. I didn't think it would have reached the point that it had and what I saw bowled me over. I found a fully online administration: X-Road, digital ID cards, personalised medical files. (In 2017, we still didn't have any of this in France!) There was electronic voting, genetics, a high-performing education system, tons of start ups and of course, the e-Residency programme, available to the entire world. Nearly everything surprised me but the electronic voting system blew my mind. In France (home to the wonderful minds of our country's National Cybersecurity Agency) we're told that this would never work. So why can it work so smoothly in Estonia and not in France? In my opinion, electronic voting is the beginning of direct democracy!"

---

6.   Estonia ambassador to Germany since September 2019.

As for Jean Spiri, he remembers his first visit to Estonia, soon after independence: "My first trip to Estonia was in 1995. I was a teenager and I went with my father. I remember the ramparts of Tallinn and a few old Ladas that had survived, but I also recall a moment that seemed to best illustrate the transition the country was living through: the opening of the first McDonald's. There was a very long line of people wanting to discover this symbol of the West and we joined the queue: such a symbolic Big Mac is well worth a little bit of waiting and has a particular kind of flavour.

I rediscovered Estonia much more recently in 2017, during a study trip organised by l'Atelier Europe[7], in which Violaine also participated. I was expecting to find perfect digital images, classrooms with computers and start ups, but not at all a global project for society built around the construction of a digital, service-oriented State platform. What I found remarkable was that our hosts were very accessible, even those at the highest levels, and that they all shared the same enthusiasm and had all developed a vision for the future of the Nation-State in the digital era. This echoed my own thinking about public transformation in France and about the threats posed to our Nation-States by solutionism, and I felt that there was something new and tremendously inspiring to be found in Estonia. I hadn't experienced this feeling of radical newness since a study trip I'd taken to Silicon Valley. This was another Silicon Valley, with values that were completely different, but just as disruptive."

---

7.   A French think tank.

We came away from the interviews we conducted with the conviction that it would be pointless to treat Estonia as an idealized model. Its geography, history, culture and the mindset of its inhabitants go a long way to explain how this model has been built. Clearly, this is where our exploration of Estonia had to begin.

We're inviting you to discover this country, its ways of thinking and its achievements, alongside numerous experts, political leaders and entrepreneurs, both French and Estonian. Why? Because Estonia is not a disembodied notion, but contains complexities and paradoxes that merit further exploration. Because Estonia tells us something about who we are and where we're heading, both in France and Europe. Because it's time to abandon an approach that focuses exclusively on western Europe and to understand, like Estonia, what the erasure of borders could mean for the Nation-State, the democratic futures of our societies and their social contracts in the digital age.

1. Do You Know Estonia?

Located in northern Europe, Estonia is bordered by the Baltic Sea to the west and north, Russia to the east and Latvia to the south. Over 2,000 islands form its continental territory, which has a surface area of 45,000 km² (about 17,375 mi²), and its coastline has been renowned for centuries for its holiday resorts. This small country, just opposite Finland, has a strong Nordic affiliation and usually prefers to be categorised as a Nordic country rather than a Baltic one. With its 1.3 million inhabitants, Estonia has one of the lowest population densities in Europe: 28.4 inhabitants per square kilometre. This low density will play a crucial role in the State's decision to turn toward digital solutions. The climate can be harsh, with winter temperatures reaching -20°C or less on the coldest days of the year. If you ever get the chance to walk in the streets of Tallinn during the kinds of temperatures that set loose the worst blizzards, you'll understand why Skype was created in Estonia! In the spring, it's like another country comes alive: terraces start popping up everywhere, while the midnight sun takes over the eternal evenings and frequent summer gatherings.

A history marked by occupations

In order to understand the key motivations behind how this platform-State functions, we must go back over how Estonian identity was constructed, its history and the conditions in which this State had to be created from scratch. These fundamentals have served as a taking off point for this digital champion. The State guarantees a real quality of life for its citizens and encourages them to create something of value, all while throwing itself into the future with an enlightened pragmatism.

Estonia is a gateway between Europe and Russia and, as a result, has always been coveted by the major powers of the region. None of these countries, including Denmark, Sweden, Poland, Germany, Tsarist Russia or the Soviet Union ceased in their efforts to claim it. For over 700 years, Estonia lived under the yoke of foreign occupations, so much so that its current existence might even be considered something of a historical anomaly. Nonetheless, in spite of centuries of occupation, it's through this history that a strong national identity was forged. From today's perspective, Estonia's long road to freedom seems to have conferred upon it the tools that now seem indispensable to understanding and thinking about the world in the digital era: a robust culture; resilience in the face of ordeal : the ability to make do with very little (lean production[8]), to continuously innovate, to try something and then quickly go back and start

---

8.   Lean production is a more effective and less wasteful manufacturing method.

again if the attempt proves unsuccessful; the instinct for real effectiveness that's geared toward action; the art of circumventing difficulties and transforming them into advantages; a willingness to create communities rather than impose them; and a practical understanding of hardship. The last, and by no means the least, of these tools, is a true understanding of the common good.

Putting things into historical perspective

During a colloquium on the Baltic countries, held in the Paris Senate on March 19, 2018, on the occasion of these countries having been independent for 100 years, Marek Tamm (Professor of Cultural History at Tallinn University) presented his vision of Estonian history in a talk entitled *Estonia between empires, a historical perspective*[9]. His analysis followed a rather simple framework to explain the country's history. For Marek Tamm, the destiny of his country has consistently been playing out between two empires: the Russian Empire to the East and the German Empire to the West (with a small Swedish interlude). These powers' use of successive integration and disintegration has marked Estonia's history. How did Estonia preserve its identity and language over the course of such a turbulent history? How did its people survive every attempt to conquer it, and why didn't they become Russian or German? With inhabitants who date back

---

9.   *Estonia, Latvia, Lithuania: 1918-2018* colloquium, Paris Senate, March 19, 2018.

to the most ancient peoples of Europe to have lived in the same place (nearly 11,000 years) and territory that was one of the last pagan lands to be converted through the Crusades, largely led by the Holy Roman Empire's Brothers of the Sword by order of the Pope, Estonia has in part defined itself by the several centuries' worth of occupation.

Starting in the 18th century, there were two distinct social classes that existed and had very little to do with each other. On one side, you had the elite Baltic-Germans, large landholders who spoke German. On the other, you had small farmers, reduced to serfdom, who spoke only Estonian. Up until the 19th century, the Estonian language was the main vehicle for transmitting their culture. This was the origin of the farmers' powerful oral tradition, in direct contrast to the written tradition of the conservative elites. It was also this particular social, linguistic and cultural situation that transformed the first Estonian intellectuals into de facto nationalists. Seen from this perspective, the Estonian language becomes the dominant factor in establishing the country's identity.

The Republic of Estonia was born on February 24, 1918, against practically all expectations and was followed by unprecedented cultural and economic development. World War II would lead to the loss of this independence for over 50 years, before the modern renaissance of the Estonian State.

The historian Marek Tamm divides this history into six phases.

The first is the medieval era, from the 13ᵗʰ to the 16ᵗʰ century. This period sees the influence of the Holy Roman Empire and the Christianisation of Estonia. It's during this phase that European integrations, both religious and economic, are initiated, notably through the Hanseatic League between the 12ᵗʰ and 17ᵗʰ centuries. In this way, military and religious orders ensured social and political structures.

The second phase is marked by the end of the Holy Roman Empire and Estonia's integration into the Swedish Empire between the 16ᵗʰ and 18ᵗʰ centuries.

At this time, Estonia was governed by Pontus de la Gardie. a man from the Aude region of France, Pontus was preparing for the priesthood before he radically changed direction and became a mercenary, first for France in the Piedmont region, and then in service of the King of Denmark, who was then looking to control the Baltic. After being appointed officer and placed at the head of a group of soldiers, he was captured by Swedish troops in 1565, during the Northern Seven Years' War. Ever the good mercenary, he offered his services to the Kingdom of Sweden, enjoyed royal recognition and was then named knight and governor of Estonia, of which he would become viceroy in 1575. As Commander in Chief of Sweden's troops, he would face and then defeat Ivan the Terrible during the Battle of Narva (a strategic border city that then belonged to Russia) in 1581. He died in 1585 in a shipwreck in the Narva River and his body lies next to that of his wife in the Lutheran cathedral of Tallinn. This story isn't as anecdotal as it might seem: in 2013, the city of Carcassonne, prefecture of the Aude region, and Tallinn, the capital of Estonia, became twin towns, as both are fortified cities, UNESCO World Heritage Sites, and share a number of characteristics[10].

Swedish control was uncontested from 1645 onwards, but this period of dominance is seen positively by Estonians, because the King of Sweden, Charles XI, confiscated a third of the land belonging to the Baltic Germans and forbade the selling of peasants without their attached lands. The Reformation also played an important role in the development of Estonian culture by encouraging the diffusion of the Bible in vernacular Estonian, and it was at this time that the first Estonian-language texts emerged. Despite the survival of paganism, the Swedish occupation also helped cement Martin Luther's doctrine, as the first surge of literacy training for peasants was put into effect in the parishes.

The third phase, according to Marek Tamm, extends from the 18th to the 20th century, when the Swedish Empire split up, to the great benefit of the Russian Empire. From 1710 onwards, following the Great Northern War, Estonia became a Russian territory. A significant move toward Estophilia emerged and expanded, so that around 1850, many intellectuals (called Estophiles) defended the use of the Estonian language and claimed a cultural identity that would

---

10. In 2013, during the signing ceremony that confirmed the cities' twin status, the Estonian ambassador to France joked that while Tallinn was called "the Carcassonne of the North", Carcassonne had yet to be referred to as "the Tallinn of the South". *Indépendant*, April 27, 2013, "Carcassonne officiellement unie à Tallinn sa sœur du Nord" [Carcassonne is officially united with Tallinn, its sister to the North].

act as a breeding ground for the future creation of an independent State. This national vision, resting as it did on the 19th century German Idealist philosopher Johann Gottlieb Fichte's definition of culture, brings with it a strong claim of belonging to two much wider spheres: the Nordic world and European civilisation.

"Let us be Estonians and let us also become Europeans, so as to become ourselves", wrote the intellectual and Young Estonian figure, Gustav Suits, at the beginning of the 20th century[11]. Belonging to the Nordic world presented itself through a "Nordic spirit" that was characterised by individualism, tolerance, democracy and ethics. The most spectacular advance would be the progressive abolition of serfdom between 1804 and 1819, before the rest of the Russian Empire. Literacy, a consequence of Swedish and Lutheran heritage, would also rapidly progress: by around 1850, 90% of Estonians over the age of 10 could read[12].

The fourth phase takes place at the start of the 20th century, from the disintegration of the Russian Empire in November 1917, to the creation of Estonia on February 24, 1918. Language remained the main transmitter of national identity. In 1918, when Estonian became the official language, it was "a revolution for a peasant idiom", according to the historian Jean-Pierre Minaudier[13]. Nonetheless,

---

11. Jean-Pierre Minaudier, *Histoire de l'Estonie et de la nation estonienne* [History of Estonia and the Estonian Nation], L'Harmattan, 2007.

12. Ibid.

13. *Histoire de l'Estonie et de la nation estonienne*, L'Harmattan, 2007.

from 1918 to 1939, the first Estonian Republic would become a semi-authoritarian regime, especially starting in 1934, during the "silent era", which earned its name because of prevailing censorship. The economic situation was difficult, but the measures taken were effective. Agrarian reform, based on the confiscation of large land holdings from Baltic Germans, would create a new generation of small landowners, while the exploitation of peat deposits and oil shale fields soared and the lumber industry also took off.

On February 21, 1918, the country officially adopted the blue, black and white flag (representing the sky, earth and snow, respectively), which had been designed by a student association in Tartu and was consecrated on June 4, 1884. There is a lively annual celebration for the flag, which was illegal during the Soviet occupation. The national anthem of 1918 ("Mu isamaa, mu õnnjarõõm") was adopted in 1869, over 50 years before independence.

The Tallinn University of Technology was founded in the same year (1918), and all university courses were taught in Estonian. The culture kept making advances, illiteracy was eradicated and by 1935, Estonia had reached the standard of living enjoyed by Finland. This remarkable success story from the interwar period spread to the following generations and remains firmly anchored in the country's collective memory.

The fifth period is that of integration into the Soviet Empire, from 1939 to 1991. The Soviet invasion in the spring of 1940 swept away the first Estonian Republic. In the secret protocols attached to the German-Soviet

Pact of August 23, 1939, Estonia is, in effect, attributed to the Russian sphere of influence. This first occupation was marked by deportations (close to 10,000 people, including women and children) and mass executions. In one year, 80,000 Soviet soldiers were stationed in Estonia: one soldier for every 12 Estonians. All members of government were executed and a third of Estonians sent to Siberia were children. In just a few months, the economy was Sovietised and the standard of living reduced to nothing. From July to October of 1941, the German invasion brought deportations to a halt but cost over 6,000 people their lives, close to a quarter of them Jews or Roma.

In 1944, the Red Army invaded Estonia yet again. At the end of the Second World War, the country had lost 20% of its population, and close to half of its industrial base was annihilated. Stalinist principles were immediately applied and by 1947, there was not a single private business left and all business relationships outside of the USSR were strictly forbidden. A resistance movement was organised, in the hopes of an Anglo-Saxon intervention which, ultimately, would never happen. In 1949, within five days, over 20,000 Estonians, among them whole families, were deported to Siberia. Between 1945 and 1949, 9% of the population was arrested, deported or shot. All survivor testimonies from this time recall the fear of being awoken in the middle of the night, never to return.

This occupation was an enormous source of trauma for Estonia even if it wasn't the Soviet republic with the lowest standard of living. At least a sixth of its population was arrested, deported or exiled. One of the lasting effects of these repressive policies is that today, there are 51 men for every 100 women over the age of 65, as opposed to, for example, France, where there are 75 men for every 100 women.

Simultaneously, the Russian language was imposed and the Russianisation of the country was reinforced with the settlement of new Russian-speaking populations. Ethnic Estonians, who accounted for 88% of the population in 1934, represented a mere 61.5% in 1989. With the acceleration of Russianisation campaigns up until the 1970s, Estonians felt that their very existence was being threatened and they feared losing their most precious national resource, which had always been their most unifying one as well: their language.

The sixth and last phase corresponds to the end of the Soviet Empire, and the subsequent drawing closer to Europe (from 1991 to today).

At the end of 1986, the first effects of perestroika brought about a loosening of censorship. Ecology became the main mobilising and unifying subject for Estonians, in whose lives nature occupies a vital position. Demonstrations were organised against the opening of new phosphate mines and in October 1987, Moscow renounced the installation of a new thermal power plant. The demonstrations then took on a more political turn and demanded a return to autonomy for the country. During the rallies that increasingly defied the central Soviet power, Estonians demonstrated their talent for getting around obstacles: the national flag was forbidden, and thus dangerous, so a few women dressed themselves in the flag's colours, while in Tartu, in 1988, a massive demonstration showcased three flags erected side by side, one blue, one black and one white.

In September 1988, the language and culture were used to demonstrate the Estonian people's yearning for independence: the national anthem was sung in public for the first time in 50 years on Tallinn's Song Festival Grounds, where 300,000 people, or close to a quarter of the population, were gathered. Leading political figures were present and the public heard the first calls for the restoration of the country's independence. Today known as the Singing Revolution, this period saw several demonstrations adopt a format that tapped into the traditional Estonian Song Festival. The emphasis on culture was one of the most remarkable strategic dimensions of the non-violent Estonian independence movement: the country's music and rich choral tradition played a central role in the upholding of unity, defiance and hope.

The Estonian Communist Party that was in power quickly joined the movement to reclaim greater autonomy and on November 16, 1988, the government adopted a declaration of sovereignty. From then on, the non-violent independence movement escalated. On August 23, 1989—50 years to the day since the signing of the German-Soviet pact—in order to attract the attention of international media outlets, 2 million people (among them children, young adults and senior citizens) from Estonia, Latvia and Lithuania joined hands to form a giant human chain across the three countries.[14] Covering over 600 kilometres, from

---

14. « Comment les tats baltes ont-ils réclamé leur indépendance grâce à une chaîne humaine record ? »[How did the Baltic States reclaim their

27

Tallinn to Vilnius, this network of people was dubbed the "Baltic Chain" and was the biggest human chain ever organised in the name of freedom. Later added to UNESCO's Memory of the World Register, this singular peaceful demonstration played a key role in the fall of the Iron Curtain.

During the next two years, the mass gatherings continued and a series of parallel institutions, including the Estonian Congress, were set up in order to rebuild an independent State from scratch.

However, in August 1991, after a coup d'état in Moscow, Soviet tanks rolled into Estonia in a desperate attempt to quell the freedom movements. The Estonian Congress and the Soviet Supreme of the Estonian Soviet Socialist Republic formally rejected the Russian coup and immediately declared the country's independence. Estonians formed human shields around radio and TV stations, including Tallinn's broadcasting tower, to prevent Soviet forces from seizing them. The failure of the coup in Moscow on August 20 would push Russia to formally recognise the independence of Estonia, and Boris Yeltsin would confirm it on August 21.

The independence of 1991 is considered to be more of a liberation, so it's the independence of 1918 that's officially celebrated. The Constitution, approved by referendum on June 28, 1992, established a Parliamentary Republic, with a single-chamber legislative body, called the *Riigikogu*, whose 101 members are

---

independence with a record-breaking human chain?] Boris Egorov, fr.rbth.com, August 15, 2018.

elected through direct, universal and proportional voting and serve four-year terms.

The last Soviet troops left the territory in 1994, as the current Estonian president recalled in September 2019: "For Estonia, World War II actually ended only 25 years ago, when the last vehicles containing the occupying troops' hardware left our soil. The outbreak of war meant for our people, our nation, and the state, more than half a century of suffering, economic regress, and absence of freedom".[15]

Tabula rasa, off with the Soviet years

Unlike the other former Soviet Socialist republics, Estonia opted for a clean break from the previous administrative system. This desire, expressed by one part of the political class, stemmed from the fact that many of the country's civil servants were Russian speakers, mostly from the Soviet Union, who had never learned Estonian. The national construction of the country relied once again on language, and so logic dictated that a new generation of local civil servants would have to take over. Estonia considered its annexation into the USSR as an invasion, and thus a digression, and so it felt keenly the need to leave behind that administrative system and to mark a far more radical break with the past than was being done in the other former Soviet republics. The subsequent economic policies followed the same model: swift

---

15. "President: World War Two only ended 25 years ago, for Estonia", ERR. ee, September 2, 2019.

privatisations, return of properties to their former owners, the liquidation of *sovkhozes* and *kolkhozes* (state-owned farms and collective farms) and the restoration of individual farms.

Marek Tamm's interpretive framework places today's Estonia in the sphere of the European empire, whose domestic market and multinational ensemble the country has joined. The term "empire" here ought to be qualified: according to former Prime Minister Siim Kallas, unlike empires in the classic political sense of the word, the European Union is essentially a voluntary membership circle, which would explain the group's hatred for the Soviets.

Marek Tamm also emphasises that Estonia's destiny has always depended on the integrations and disintegrations of empires. For him, this means that it's very unlikely that Estonia will be able to control its destiny, so the country must make the most of the current situation. Doubtless, this sheds light on why membership in the European Union is, while not impassioned, deeply rooted: according to the results of the September 2017 Eurobarometer survey, only 11% of Estonians have an unfavourable view of the EU, compared to 21% in other European countries.

2. A Strong Identity Rooted in Cultural Practices

Singing, the great unifier of the Estonian soul

One older Estonian woman told us, "The most important thing to understand about our history, is our tradition of singing". While singing in a choir is an integral part of a child's development, singing festivals have always played a leading role in the sharing and spreading of national sentiment: the first singing demonstration was organised while under Russian domination in 1869 to celebrate the 50th anniversary of the abolition of serfdom. Ever since then, the Estonian love of singing has expressed itself in large concerts, and singing festivals have become the main form of community celebration, as they help maintain a strong connection to Estonian identity. This custom relies on traditional songs which speak of the love of nature, flowers and the forest, as well as secular legends that have survived Christianity, and which evoke a pantheon of gods, including the god of thunder and the goddess of the sea and nature. Even the Soviet regime maintained this tradition, seeing

31

it as a way to control minds by reinforcing a certain kind of Soviet patriotism under the guise of national communion. "My Country is My Love", written by the great 19th century poetess Lydia Koidula, is the most famous Estonian song. Its popularity was restored in the 1960s, when it became a sort of unofficial national anthem. At the beginning of the 19th century, the Estonian Song Festival (*Laulupidu*) was included on the UNESCO Intangible Cultural Heritage List. Every five years, about 40,000 choir members perform in front of close to 250,000 spectators. Violaine Champetier de Ribes took part in the last Festival, at the beginning of July 2019. She explains: "This is an essential experience for anyone who wants to understand the Estonian soul. There was something very special about the gathering together of all these choristers, anywhere between the ages of 5 and 90, some of whom had come from practically the other end of the earth. I have never witnessed such a display of national fervour that was entirely stripped of any political connotation. I didn't understand the words, but I was still blown away by the sometimes tribal-sounding melodies, as well as the joy and emotion of the crowd. Almost everyone was in traditional dress and had a mobile phone in their hands. This demonstration epitomises the special Estonian alchemy that so effectively links tradition with modernity."

Poker Face

One of the most striking Estonian characteristics is the famous poker face. During your first encounter with an Estonian, you won't know where you stand, if they're happy or not to see you. This attitude comes, in part, from the traditional distrust of foreigners but is also due to reserve, withdrawal and shyness. Once the ice is broken however, relations will become entirely agreeable and cordial. Estonians are introverted, going out of their way to avoid crowds and lines, and in his book *Estonians Inside Out*[1], Lauri Vhatre goes so far as to suggest that the true reason for the success of digital administration might be the Estonian aversion to interacting with or being close to one another, and that scientists should look into the subject. Of course, the country's opening up to the world and numerous international exchanges encourage today's population to be a bit more forthcoming.

The cult of nature

It's impossible to talk about Estonia without mentioning its population's attachment to nature. It's almost as if their unconscious has preserved ancestral beliefs that all plants, minerals and animals have spirits. Is this a kind of syncretism, reminiscent of animism and paganism? It's hard to tell. When you ask an Estonian what their religion is, some reply "nature", because the country has no official state religion. The guide who took us around the old town of Tallinn in 2017 told us, with a big smile: "We speak to trees and we hug them, although I can't remember the last time I did that." There's nothing like a weekend in the

---

1. Lauri Vahtre, *Estonians Inside Out*, Pilgrim, 2017.

country, with long walks in the woods or marshes and mushroom picking! Forests cover close to half of the country and are part of Estonian identity, and respect for nature is taught to children when they're very young. In 2008, Estonians even launched a civic movement called "Let's Do It": 50,000 Estonians rolled up their sleeves to clean up the country in five hours. Since then, 120 countries and 20 million people have joined in this annual endeavour, which is now referred to as World Clean up Day.

Sauna as a practice

Saunas are an important part of social life in countries like Estonia, Finland, Latvia and Russia. While the oldest public sauna was opened in Tallinn in 1310, the origins of this practice date back to 2000 B.C. in northern Europe.

In ancient Estonian society, saunas occupied a central function in health and hygiene: they were where you were born, where you spent your adulthood and even your last days. Under Soviet occupation, relaxation rooms were added to saunas, so that between sessions and hidden from the state's surveillance apparatus, people could exchange food and drink and even conduct under-the-table negotiations. Today, the largest sauna marathon in Europe takes place in the Estonian town of Otepää, and the famous smoked sauna of Võru has been recognized on the UNESCO list of cultural heritage.

For Anni Oviir, founder of Estonian Saunas, Estonian entrepreneurial success stories like Skype and Transferwise can be attributed to the presence of saunas in the office: "Saunas have never just been rooms. They are a way of life and so, in many ways, the history of the sauna is really a history of us."[2]

2.　"Here's why the history of the sauna is deeper than you might think: Saunas were built for survival before becoming intertwined with the lives of the people who used them", *Medium*, March 18, 2018.

3. A State is Born

Starting from a blank page

Despite a half-century of Soviet occupation and Russianisation, Estonians succeeded in preserving their language, culture and their idea of the nation, all of which make up a single notion that we might call "Estonianism". In 1991, the country faced a significant challenge: to build, and not merely modernise, their State, while making a clean break with the past. At the same time, the first national budgets were greatly reduced and the government had to figure out a way to create an administration in a country with low population density and vast uninhabited areas, without the means to massively recruit civil servants or invest in the construction of public buildings.

While the Soviet Union was splitting up in 1991, Estonia found itself in a time warp. "We had nothing," recalls General Riho Terras, Commander of the Estonian Armed Forces and former student activist. "The country had to restart things from scratch." To that end, each citizen received the equivalent of

€10 or \$10.60. "That was it," concludes the General, laughing. "We each began with 10 Euros!"[1]

The foundation for construction

Parliamentary and presidential elections took place on September 20, 1992, with a participation rate of 68%. Lennart Meri won the presidential election and held that office until 2001 (he died in 2006). His life bears the marks of Estonian history. Born in 1929 in Tallinn, this son of a diplomat was educated in multiple countries, including the Lycée Janson-de-Sailly in Paris. He was deported with his family to Siberia in 1941, where from the age of 12, he was put to work in the forest. After returning to Estonia, he earned a doctorate in History in 1953. Before being elected president, he was a writer and a filmmaker, and then Minister of Foreign Affairs from 1990 to 1992. As president, he chose Mart Laar, a young 32-year-old historian and founder of the Christian Democratic Party, to be his prime minister.

Shock therapy

Mart Laar's government implemented a string of drastic measures, known as "shock therapy", and in doing so, put into effect one of the most radical economic liberalisation political programmes that had

---

1. "Is This Tiny European Nation a Preview of Our Tech Future?",*Fortune*, April 27, 2017.

ever been seen in the former Eastern Bloc countries. This programme proved successful and since 1995, the Estonian economy has enjoyed renewed growth. Oil shale resources have been crucial to this prosperity and the country's energy industry, which was created after the Second World War, produced the majority of electricity in the 1990s, thus ensuring a precious energy independence. Another pioneering measure was implemented in 1994, when Estonia became the first country in the world to impose a flat tax of 26% on individuals and a corporate flat tax of 20% on profits that are not reinvested.

Previous experiences of an independent State

The experience of being independent from 1918 to 1940 greatly contributed to how construction in a working State was approached. Dominique Dubarry[2] has returned to Estonia on many occasions since his first trip there in January 1992 and recalls: "I met people who had lived through deportations and population displacements. Most had been sent to Siberia when they were children. But their grandparents had passed on the memory of the 1918 independence. The return of Estonians raised in exile also played a role in the country's reconstruction."

The geographic proximity to Finland has been crucial. The two countries' languages are similar (both

2.   Author of *France - Pays baltes.La force d'une relation trop lointaine* [France – Baltic Countries. The Strength of a Very Remote Relationship], Félix Torres Éditeur, 2010.

are Finno-Ugric languages) and, during the Soviet occupation, northern Estonia was steeped in Finnish culture through television shows that familiarised the public with notions of freedom and the market economy. Kadi Metsandi Economic Counsellor to the Estonian Embassy in Paris from 2015 to 2018[3], recalls that Estonians, who have freedom in their DNA, were heavy consumers of Radio Free Europe.[4] When the Soviets outlawed antennas, the Estonian population used thermometers to catch Finnish TV waves. Moscow, observing the heightened demand for thermometers in stores, began raising serious questions about the health of the Estonians. This is the kind of tactic that Estonians are referring to when they talk about "risk-taking Estonia"!

After independence, in order to catch up to the rest of the world in terms of technology and finance, Estonia naturally turned to Finland and Scandinavia for all of its technology and financial investment questions. In return, Finnish and Swedish companies expected to be able to communicate with modern tools, meaning e-mail, not faxes.

The role of banks

The transition to a free-market economy provoked the explosion of commercial banking offers, which had been non-existent until then. The players in the

---

3. Currently Director of Development Cooperation and Humanitarian Aid at Estonian Foreign Ministry
4. Interview with the authors.

banking world immediately chose to use innovative online services. Facing the same problems as the administration, they didn't even consider opening banking agencies in a country with such low population density: they collaborated with public authorities and in 1996, a year after the first governmental website was launched, they opened the first online bank, which drew over 20,000 clients in less than six months.

In order to avoid the risks of fraud and identity theft, the two main banking establishments in the country (Hansapank and EestiÜhispank) worked with telephone service providers to create an authentication centre for online payments. This technology would be used again for administrative processes.[5]

Visionary political leaders

In 1995, Toomas Hendrik Ilves, then Minister of Foreign Affairs, read Jeremy Rifkin's controversial book, *The End of Work*[6], and understood that the large-scale computerisation taking place throughout the world would bring the number of available jobs down considerably. Ilves and his colleagues saw an opportunity: in a small, newly independent country like Estonia, computers could quickly make up for an

5.   "Estonie, se reconstruire par le numérique"[Estonia: RebuildingItself ThroughDigitalTechnology], Renaissance numérique, 2015.

6.   Jeremy Rifkin,*The End of Work: The Decline of the Global Labor Force and the Dawn of the Post-Market Era*, Putnam Publishing Group, 1995.

insufficient labour force and a chronically lacking physical infrastructure.[7]

Born in Stockholm in 1953 to Estonian parents who fled Soviet occupation in 1940, Ilves is one of the pillars of the construction of modern Estonia. He lived for a long time in the United States where, at the beginning of the 1970s, he studied Psychology at Columbia University and then the University of Pennsylvania. Deeply influenced by the computer science classes he took in his childhood, he was convinced of the importance of teaching code to very young children. After returning to Europe in the 1980s, he worked at Radio Free Europe from 1984 to 1993, and then became Estonian Ambassador to the United States, Canada and Mexico. He served twice as Minister of Foreign Affairs, became a Member of the European Parliament in 2004, then First Vice-President of the Commission for Foreign Affairs in the European Parliament. In 2006, he was elected president of Estonia and held this position until 2016.

Very young teams

As a 20-year-old student, Kaidi Ruusalepp, now CEO of the Fintech start up Funderbeam, was recruited by the Estonian government to be the first IT law advisor for the new technologies administration, and co-authored the Estonian Digital Signatures Act of 2000."I had no law degree and no understanding

---

7. "How tiny Estonia stepped out of old USSR's shadow to become an internet titan", *The Guardian*, 2012.

of technology", she admits. Her first task was to create a law around digital signatures, years before most governments were even interested in the subject. "We wanted to change the country. We had our minds and we had to make the most of them." The model for a modern government, one that was paperless, effective and avant-garde, emerged along with the creation of a new State.

Siim Kallas, economist and president of the Central Bank, was part of the first working groups that helped prepare the country for independence. He recalls that the team in charge of this initiative had less than 10 people, all very young, who had to invent everything! The strength of the Estonian character made possible this kind of State building, what Siim Kallas calls the mindset of doers, as well as a predisposition to readily accept niche ideas.

Mart Laar was Prime Minister of Estonia from 1992 to 1994 and again from 1999 to 2002. In 2007, he revisited his experiences in an article for the think tank The Heritage Foundation.

Here are some excerpts[8]:

"It was cold in Estonia in January 1992. The end of Communism had led to real chaos in the country. The stores were completely empty and the Russian ruble no longer had any value. Industrial production had dropped by over 30%, more than during the Great Depression of the 1930s. Real wages had fallen by 45%,

---

8. The authors would like to thank The Heritage Foundation for the partial reproduction of this article.

while global inflation had passed 1000% and the price of fuel had risen by more than 10,000%.

[...]

We were totally dependent on Russia, which represented 92% of our overseas trade. We didn't have much to sell on the global markets. The Soviet economy had destroyed the environment and our infrastructures were in catastrophic condition.

[...]

In June of 1992, we launched our monetary reforms by becoming the first country in the former Soviet Union to create its own currency. This reform programme had been established with the help of multiple foreign think tanks: The Heritage Foundation, the International Republican Institute, the Adam Smith Institute and Timbro, in Sweden. The first Estonian think tanks, created years prior by the parties who had just come to power, played equally vital roles. Most of the programme was presented and discussed during events organised by these task forces, which allowed the public to become more familiar with the details. Without these task forces, the swift and effective creation of a government action plan would probably not have been possible.

[...]

The members of the government were very young, just like me, the newly elected Prime Minister: I was 32 and many other ministers were even younger. Like most young people, we didn't know what was possible and what wasn't—so we did impossible things. We passed a huge number of necessary laws in a few months and we balanced the budget. After that, we passed a law that said only balanced budgets could be presented to the Estonian Parliament. This requirement allowed the government to then pass similar budgets more easily and made budgetary balance integral to how Estonia was run.

[...]

The reduction of subsidies sent a simple and clear message to the industrial Soviet dinosaurs: "Start working or get out." As we would soon see, the majority chose to work. Starting in 1993, we saw the first real results of these measures. The macro-economic situation stabilised. The rate of inflation went down considerably, from 1000% in 1992 to 89.8% in 1993 (it would reach 29% in 1995). The economy was redirected, going from East to West, and exports started to rise rapidly. This galvanised people, made them move, forced them to make decisions and to take on their responsibilities. The government declared that it could only help those who were ready to do something for themselves. This was unpopular, but it helped change attitudes.

[...]

For an economy in transition like Estonia's, attracting foreign investments proved to be a better alternative to accepting loans from international institutions like the World Bank or the IMF (International Monetary Fund). If we had taken development aid, we would have risked staying behind. That kind of help often relies on obsolete technology and out-dated recommendations that modern countries don't use and by choosing this assistance, countries in transition lose the possibility of using their lateness as a kind of springboard for development. Put bluntly, our response was: 'Don't give us help; give us more opportunities to do business.'

Certain countries try to encourage foreign investors by offering all sorts of incentives, tax exemptions, privileges, special rights, etc. But the alternative is to create a business environment that supports both local and international investment, without making a distinction between the two. This is the path that Estonia chose.

In a short period of time, between 1993 and 1994, we'd gone from a country that was practically invisible or unknown to a kind of Eldorado for foreign investors. The systematic efforts of the government to build our global reputation for excellence played a decisive role in that process. This was so successful that by the second half of the 1990s, Estonia was welcoming more foreign investments per inhabitant than any other country in Central and Eastern Europe. This massive influx of money allowed us to create new workspaces and develop our knowledge and technologies; in short, to make our country more modern and more competitive.

[...]

An important step in this regard was initiating dialogue between management and labour in Estonia. Three-party negotiations were led between the State, employers and employees and in 1992 and 1993, the government supported the transformation of trade unions from how they had been under the Soviet Union into free trade unions.

[...]

No radical reform would have been possible without laws governing the economic sphere. However, good laws alone aren't enough. Developing economies need effective institutions that help new laws move from theory to practice. Formal legal systems make judges, prosecutors, arbitrators, officers of the court, private legal professions, etc. the primary interpreters and performers of laws. Developing and securing all of the systems that govern these laws is just as vital for the success of reforms as is the creation of an effective civil service.

[...]

The pre-eminence of the law is fundamental to the fight against corruption, one of the worst plagues on economies in transition. Our experience shows that the most effective way to combat corruption and organised crime is to place a market economy in civil society, within the framework of rule of law. To that end, we've paid particular attention to the reform of our banking system. Banks are key to the economy and if organised crime takes control of them, it can then quickly seize control of the entire country. Money laundering, dirty money and any other criminal operation must be cut from the banking system as soon as possible. Our government is extremely vigilant and firm on this question, with dirty money always being a warning sign of the arrival of dishonest individuals.

The Estonian tax system had to be simple, inexpensive to implement, transparent and comprehensible to tax payers, with as large a tax base as possible, and exemptions reduced to the maximum, much like incentives for tax avoidance, including the underground economy. Taxes also had to stay low in order to encourage activity and create more growth.

The best way to reach all of these objectives at once was to place a flat tax on each person's revenue, which we introduced on January 1, 1994. In 1992, Estonia had around 2,000 companies. By the end of 1994, this number had climbed to 70,000! We'd gone from a working-class country to a country of entrepreneurs. The incentives to take charge of their own futures had, in the end, helped Estonians avoid massive unemployment.

[...]

The radical business reforms of the 15 years following liberation transformed Estonia from what it had been during the Soviet era. It's sometimes difficult for us to remember how the country used to be. Estonia was, in fact, the first formerly Communist country to reach the status of a "free" economy in the annual Index of Economic Freedom, released by The Heritage Foundation and *The Wall Street Journal*. What is still more remarkable is that it wasn't just a "free" economy but "one of the most free" in the world, since we were ranked 12th in the 2007 Index of Economic Freedom.

All of these changes helped us prepare for the new challenges of the 21st century. Our nation has made a real leap in contemporary technology and is a leader in digital governance, which can be a very effective tool in creating an open and agile administration.

Our government's use of the internet has been a driving force in the creation of new high-tech players in Estonia, which has become the birthplace of several technology companies. The most famous Estonian invention is Skype, a video-conferencing and instant messaging system, which in 2006 was voted the third most influential brand in the world. Of course, there is still a lot of work left to do, and new challenges await us, but the hardest years are behind us.

To return to this transition period that saw us passing from poverty to prosperity in a few years, the experience that I've drawn from it is that the task of the Prime Minister is not to be popular but to form a work alliance, to have a clear programme and to make decisions.

Of course, implementing such reforms can make a government unpopular, and might even lead to its removal from power. That's not important. What matters is being able to positively transform the country, without expecting recognition for doing so. With a little perspective, we can acknowledge, 'it was a dirty job, but someone had to do it'. Once set in motion, the train can't be stopped easily. And this, in the end, is the only thing that counts."

This statement from the former Prime Minster, while also a defence of his track record (of very liberal policies), helps us better understand how a modern, digital State was born.

There remains, nevertheless, a mystery, or at least, something unsaid: how did Estonians understand that a digital State would be the ideal solution at a time when the internet just barely existed? Certainly, many of the country's features lend themselves to the idea, like the very low population density in certain regions, which would make the roll-out of public services throughout the entire country very costly. (There are only 1.3 Estonians living in an area that is more spread out than Belgium or the Netherlands.) However, it would also have needed the technical skills to implement and successfully deploy the concept. According to Siim Kallas[9], it was the US which offered Estonia a ready-to-use IT system when it was looking for State-building solutions. Others say it was Finland that made the offer. In any case, the already existent systems were too expensive for Estonia: they cost more than the total budget of the young State! So, it held onto the digital public infrastructure idea proposed by foreign countries, but decided to build its own IT system, with its own top-level engineers.

During the Soviet era, Estonia was home to a cybernetics institute that had been created in 1960, a place that Dominique Dubarry remembers well: "At the end of the 1980s, there were a lot of Estonians who worked in the IT management of factories in the USSR. They returned to their country in 1991 and their departure contributed to the economic collapse of the Soviet Union."[10]

In an interview for an Australian publication, Siim Sikkut, CIO of the Estonian government, adds: "We had research centres and leading IT during the Soviet era. We used them to create the first businesses, which began working for the banks and for the government. From here, we focused on technological expertise, but declined in other areas."[11] Tarvi Martens, an information systems architect, today supervises the country's

9. President of the Central Bank, Prime Minster from 2002 to 2003, EU Commissioner from 2001 to 2014.

10. Op. cit.

11. "Creating a digital society: Can Australia learn something from Estonia?" cio.com, February 17, 2018.

digital voting programme. In a *New Yorker* article[12], he recalls: "For decades, Estonia has systematically looked to digital technology in order to resolve its administrative difficulties. In 1970, one of the State's projects even used the coupling of computerised data to help single people find their soul mates, 'for the good of the popular economy'." In the Soviet model of the division of labour, Estonia held the position of expert in "new technologies", and its first computers date from 1959. "The Cybernetics Institute of the Tallinn University of Technology was at the cutting edge of the field, well before independence. So much so that in 1997, it gave birth to one of our biggest R&D centres: Cybernetica", recalls Jaan Priisalu, head of government cybersecurity. In 1992, he was one of the first scholars of the new regime to get a Master of Philosophy in Fundamental Computer Science in Toulouse. He then worked in banking, before joining the Estonian civil service[13].

Thanks to its technological prowess, as well as its engineers, Estonia has succeeded in finding the right resources.

The first internet connections were made in 1992 at university facilities in Tallinn and Tartu. After the privatisation of the State monopoly on telecommunications, Finnish and Swedish businesses instituted a fibre optic network that worked with modern communication services for landlines and mobile phones. French native Kevin Chavanne, a former student in

---

12. "Estonia the Digital Republic", *The New Yorker*, December 18, 2017.

13. "Bienvenue en e-Estonia" [Welcome to e-Estonia], *Les Échos*, December 1, 2014.

the Democracy and Governance Master's programme at the University of Tartu and now an investment associate at Funderbeam, effectively sums up how the State could be created on this new digital basis: "If Estonia was born with the internet, it's because Estonians have been bathing in it from the very beginning."[14]

However, technical skills aren't enough: you need the population on your side as well. When we met Andres Kütt, a software architect, specialist in technological strategy and digital governance, and author and lecturer, in May 2017 at the Estonian Information System Authority, he explained: "In 1991, no one knew how to lead the country. We've been able to put in place this digital administration because we didn't have the means to do otherwise. So we started small, relying on one fundamental pillar: trust. Little by little, this was established between the young geeks, new politicians, entrepreneurs and citizens. That trust went global when it resulted in new technology and effectiveness."

The steps and thought processes behind the rapid rebuilding of the country have led to a reinvented and co-built State. This success comes from the combination of a visionary government's efforts, the proactive work of the new technologies sector, and the population's interest in these technologies and support for the project.

14. Interview with the authors.

The historically opposing view: making the State transparent

Dominique Dubarry recalls: "In 1992, what struck me was the attitude of the people and their extreme poverty: they wouldn't look at me, they avoided my eyes. After two days, I learned that the green rain-coat I was wearing looked a lot like those worn by KGB agents. The fear of the people made a huge impression on me. Estonians knew that they were being listened to in their homes and on the street. For the next 18 months, meetings and conversations took place in parks because they didn't want to be overheard, and even then, you had to stop talking when someone came near you with a shopping cart or a pram. Everyone paid close attention to what was said and meticulously chose their words. Everyone was suspicious and very careful."

For Kadi Metsandi, breaking from the Soviet era was crucial. The State had to be transparent if it wanted the population to support it. That meant doing things differently: "The State is there to serve the citizens because they're the ones who vote and are elected into office, unlike during the Soviet era. We had to show that we were willing to reverse how things had been, that the State was there for the citizens. We have a small population, so we had to do this all together. The main question then was: how do we have the population accept a State that it wants, instead of a State that it's being subjected to? The response was to create the best possible context. We began with a model exclusive to us, one that made us feel good, protected and trusted. Ever since, that model has inspired others and has been exported all over the world..."[15]

The very origins of this idea came from the desire to create a "minimal and effective State". This is an avant-garde programme that increases how far IT and the internet can go and allows impressive levels of accessibility. Since the 1990s, all Estonian schools have internet and computer lab access. Digital coverage has seen considerable growth, placing Estonia at the head of the curve when it comes to internet penetration rates: 92% of users out of 1.3 million inhabitants in 2016[16].

In 1997, the government began looking at new kinds of digital documents to complement paper. Tarvi Martens was at the time directing a cybernetics and security business. When the first electronic identification cards were introduced in 2002, he was convinced that they should be mandatory and inexpensive. He understood that whoever offered the most ubiquitous and safest platform would manage the country's digital future – and that the offer should come from an elected leadership, not a Big Tech company that would be looking for the exclusive profits. "The first thing to do was to push people toward this card, without them knowing how it would serve them, and then to tell them: 'Now that you have this card, let's put a few applications on it.'"

---

15. Former Economic Counsellor to the Estonian Embassy in Paris, now Director of Development Cooperation and Humanitarian Aid at Estonian Foreign Ministry Interview with the authors.

16. *Government as a platform*, Marggetts&Naumann, 2016.

The first killer App was the one that Martens was still working on: online voting (from a computer or a mobile phone). Only 5,000 citizens had used their digital ID card for administrative tasks and in the first electronic elections in 2005, over 9,000 electronic votes were counted (only 2% of voters). In 2017, a third of all the votes were done online[17] and in 2019, that number jumped to 43.75%.

Electronic citizenship

10 years earlier, when passports and identity cards for its one million citizens were due for renewal, the government used this as an opportunity to institute a new kind of citizenship. The digital identity law of 2000 was the first in the world to create electronic citizenship. This required a unique username that would be used for all types of administrative tasks and services available online: driving licences, bank accounts, social security numbers, health services, etc. Citizens' medical files would also be accessible from a connected device[18]. In an interview for *Lifehacker*[19], former Estonian president, Toomas Hendrik Ilves, relates: "I had this kind of crazy idea, I applied Fishkin's deliberative democracy technique. You get a lot of people together to discuss issues. First all

---

17. "Estonia the Digital Republic", *The New Yorker*, December 18, 2017.

18. « Estonie, se reconstruire par le numérique » [Estonia, rebuilding itselfthrough the digital], Renaissance numérique, 2015.

19. "I'm former Estonian president Toomas Hendrik Ilves, and This is How I Work", *Lifehacker*, October 16, 2019.

together and then in small groups. You end up moving toward the centre, toward more rational decisions.

Using the ID system, we asked people to submit their proposals for reforming governance. We got lots of [opinions], and at that time we couldn't [analyse] them with machine learning yet, so we had these university professors sift through all of them and categorise them. You can only do this if [everyone] identifies themselves, to keep out trolling. Fishkin has done this around the world. You bring in a representative group, around a thousand people in our case.

We brought them in, following the demographic profile of the country, [urban and rural], different parts of the country, different ages, different ethnic groups, all that. And then they discussed all these issues. And came up with—in terms of opinion polls—some counterintuitive results. These were turned into legislative proposals. And I presented them to the parliament. Parliament voted on them. Most of them they voted down of course, but some of them they [passed], including one on the minimum size to create a political party. Which of course backfired on everyone with a liberal cast of mind, because it allowed the registration of a hard right party that now is in government."

A national political project and its consequences (inclusion, territory, education)

Linnar Viik, part-time lecturer at the Estonian IT College remembers: "We realised that if the government was going to use the internet, the internet had to be available to everybody. So we built a huge network of public internet access points for people who couldn't afford them at home."[20]Communication services thus saw rapid technological development in the 1990s and several new services came on the market, to great success. The majority of families with a middle-class standard of living considered internet access a necessity. Public internet access points provided by the State and local authorities also contributed to the growing use of computers. In 2001, 54% of the total population was using mobile phones while 10 years earlier, more than half of the population didn't even have a landline!

Tiger Leap

In 1996, Toomas Hendrik Ilves, then Estonian Ambassador to the United States, and Jaak Aaviksoo, then Minister of Education, launched a programme for schools called Tiger Leap, which would encourage the use of information and communications technology (ICT) in education. Today, all Estonian schools have high-speed network connections and a complete teaching methodology adapted to every level, while all teachers can use Virtual Learning Environments, and the State pilots research and training programmes in all areas of IT and education, online learning and digital and media culture.

---

20. "How tiny Estonia stepped out of USSR's shadow to become an internet titan", *The Guardian*, 2012.

ICT is seen by primary and secondary schools as a general teaching tool that can be used for every subject. Public and private partnerships to promote new technologies are also very much encouraged. For example, in 2012, the government launched ProgeTiger: inspired by a public-private partnership between the Tiigrihüpe Foundation, a public organisation, and the Finnish IT company Tieto, this programme encouraged students over the age of seven to learn how to code.

Most teachers have been using new technologies in their classes for almost a decade and overall, the use of ICT by Estonian professors is higher than that of the average European. This means that all levels taken together, Estonia is 1st among leading countries. Estonian secondary-school students know how to code and learn astronomy thanks to virtual reality. This digitising of education is crucial to the high marks Estonia receives in the PISA education rankings: 1st among European countries, 3rd in the world, behind Singapore and Japan. In 2006, former Estonian president, Toomas Hendrik Ilves, gave a speech where he advised: "Instead of buying a second-hand Mercedes, give your children a computer." This policy of training people from the youngest ages brings results: one Estonian student out of 10 will pursue a career in ICT, a rate that is twice higher than the OECD average.

"Even in middle school, there's a strong message: 'Don't be afraid, learn how to code even if you're a girl. If you say you're studying IT, that's the coolest thing you can do—it's your parents' dream!'"[21] says

21. "Estonia, the Skype effect", *BBC News*, May 13, 2016.

Anni-Brit Remmelg, a volunteer with the Garage 48 foundation[22]. Another interesting example of digital transformation within the Estonian education system: the e-Schoolbag project. Starting in 2020, all educational materials will be digitised and available in an online e-Schoolbag.

While Estonia is ranked 2nd in Europe (and 4thin the world) when it comes to adult literacy, with a rate of 99.8%[23], its current education system has been created to help citizens become more responsible. That's why schools have mandatory programmes in "digital competence", and there are even plans for a national exam that will test digital competence in five areas, including the correct usage of internet etiquette. "Education is two steps ahead of the labour market," explains Kristel Rillo, who runs e-services at the Ministry of Education. "Children are two steps ahead of middle-aged workers in learning how to become digital citizens."[24]Here's a model that could inspire several countries—including France—which are still behind in international rankings.

With Tiger Leap, training programmes are being administered in libraries throughout the country and include senior citizens. Road-shows have been organised everywhere in the country to present digital services: there's a real investment in communication

22. A foundation that helps launch start ups.

23. *The 2011 United Nations Development Programme (UNDP) Human Development Report.*

24. "Where in the world will you find the most advanced e-government? Estonia", ideas.ted.com, March 15, 2018.

and training, with the consistent promise that access to these services will be available everywhere in the country. Ilves recalls about this period[25]: "Fortunately we had a minister of education who really liked the idea and pushed it through the government. We had a teachers' union weekly newspaper, and they devoted at least one article or editorial to condemning me [weekly] for an entire year. But this thing took off. And by '98 or '99, all Estonian schools were online. Meanwhile the banks saw this as a great opportunity. They're always looking to cut costs. And in Estonia we have lots and lots of little villages, and each one had at least two if not three brick-and-mortar banks that were visited very rarely. It was a huge cost. So we launched a program with the banks where we went around the country and taught older people, mainly in the rural areas, how to use a computer. Part of the project was to put computers in all municipal centres, town halls, and administrative centres. People didn't own computers yet because they were expensive and people were poor. So you could go there and do all your stuff for free. We had all these little signs all over the place, [like] the standard direction signs that you have in Europe, except we had a little @ symbol, with an arrow saying something like 'Internet access point two hundred meters to the right'."

25. "I'm former Estonian president Toomas Hendrik Ilves, and This is How I Work", *Lifehacker*, October 16, 2019.

Pillars of this political project

With a high rate of internet penetration and integration of several governmental e-services in the daily lives of inhabitants and businesses, Estonia is a model of how internet accessibility can act as a driving force for the development of a human society: since 2000, the country has considered internet access a fundamental human right. Wi-Fi connections are available in thousands of public locations (and in trains), the country is covered in high-speed 3G and 4G mobile networks (meaning they're available to 85% of the population), and Tallinn is already enjoying 5G[26]. The government's objective is that by 2020, all residents of Estonia will have access to high-speed internet (30 Mbit/s) and that at least 60% of homes will be using ultra-high-speed internet (100 Mbit/s).

As Taavi Kotka, former CEO of Nortal and former CIO of the government, reminds us: "The idea wasn't to become a digital country. More than anything, this was a political project: to best serve all citizens." The development of this information society was founded on the essential principles that Parliament adopted in 1998. Here are a few of them:

• The protection of fundamental rights and liberties, as well as personal information and data relating to identity must be ensured.

• Individuals are the owners of their personal information and they control how it's used.

---

26. National programme for the development of digital infrastructures.

- The public sector must organise its processes so that citizens, businesses and public entities enter their personal information only once.
- The information society is developed in cooperation with public, private and third-party sectors, as well as any other concerned party, including users of ICT solutions.
- The information society has been created for all residents of Estonia, with particular attention paid to the integration of social groups presenting specific needs, to regional development and to support for local initiatives.
- Internet access must be guaranteed for everyone.

"Innovation is an ecosystem that relies on an attitude, a mindset and a culture"[27]

Marten Kaevats, the government's National Digital Advisor, returns to the fundamentals of how a digital society is built: "It's a culture of openness and trust, rather than an accumulation of gadgets; you need time to have this mindset. In 2018, our country celebrated its 100th anniversary. In one century, we Estonians have shown ourselves to be rather inventive—even during a time of penury, we knew how to find, not just solutions, but disruptive solutions. However, in the last 20 years, we've became attached to the idea of building a digital society that offers everyone the chance to be transparent and worthy of

27. Marten Kaevats.

trust and which favours the spirit of enterprise. And this culture here is the creator of opportunities, for Estonians and foreigners. The tools that we use are changing our ways of thinking, the passage to the digital signifies a constant upgrading of the individual, each person must adapt themselves regularly, under the algorithms, adjust their attitudes. It's not easy to evolve, and changing the nature of an entire society is even more difficult. However, it's inevitable if we want to stay resilient in a global context that is always evolving. Business as usual isn't an option. Here, disruption is part of our national education programme and everyone who's interested must learn to adapt themselves to change. The mission of the government is to accompany this continuous evolution by maintaining a healthy balance between the ideal and the real."[28]

For Toomas Hendrik Ilves[29]:"The most fundamental aspect of digitisation of society is, how governance is turned up side-down. Bureaucracy has always been a sequential process. Digitisation allows parallel processing. (...)You get in this mindset, once you get out of the 5,000-year history of a bureaucracy. In a digital world, [identity] is not necessarily tied to geographical location. (...)This goes back to my main point about digitisation: it's not about digitisation. (...)It's all political and regulatory."

---

28. Estonian Government, *Life in Estonia*, February 2018.
29. "I'm former Estonian President ToomasHendrikIlves, and This is How I Work", *Lifehacker*, October 16, 2019.

Last but certainly not least, Siim Sikkut[30]shares his insights about what it takes to lead a successful digital transformation: "In digital transformation, we should be ready to change whatever the current practice or law is. This is the core factor in being able to experiment and change how we do things. It's important to consider change management and how we get people on-board; and, most importantly, how we communicate. 'It's never been about technology. It's always about how we re-design, how we transform and how we operate as a Government.'"[31]

It's this history and these grand principles that helped spark the construction of the original model of Estonia's e-government. In 2017, *Wired* magazine called Estonia the most advanced digital society in the world. This ranking is a good reflection of the work undertaken over the last 25 years: it's not just the construction of a digital State, but also the acculturation of a whole society. To return to the words of Antoine Picron in his report for the Institut Sapiens[32], "the reduction of the digital gap has unquestionably been an essential element in the Estonian digital transition, as it allows for the comprehension, democratisation and effectiveness of the e-Government model".[33]

---

30. According to the NGO Apolitical, Siim Sikkut, the chief information officer of the Estonian government, is one of 2019's most influential people in digital government.

31. "Building the Digital Government – Estonia's Digital Transformation", Under the Hood, October 26, 2019.

32. French Think tank

33. *L'e-Estonie, modèle d'un étatplateforme e-gouverné* [E-Estonia, model of an e-governed platform-state], Institut Sapiens, July 2018.

4. The Estonian Platform-State: How Does it Work?

The founding principles of the Estonian digital State

The construction of the digital State that is Estonia relies not only on the organising principles linked to technology but also on political imperatives: transparency and effectiveness in the public sector, orientation toward client-citizens, the effective protection of personal information and resistance to digital fracture.

Observing this digital State through the lens of technology alone would be a mistake. Certainly, its particular digital architecture partly explains its success, but it's also because its conception was based on the needs of its citizens and a global vision of what a modern State should be. For Andres Kütt, "Basically, all of this relies on your conception of what it means to govern a country."[1] And for Estonians,

---

1. Information architect and expert in technological strategy and digital governance. Interview with the authors.

it means, "the State is us", referring to the primacy of the citizens and, "Country as a service". What's important isn't the administration as creator of the State but the State getting meaning from the service and added value that it brings to its people.

This is where we get the birth of a system that is focused on the user, the simplicity of using it and being a true platform of services for the citizen. It's inspired by UX (user experience) design: the user experience of the citizen is at the centre of all reflections. This movement has now affected all businesses might seem too modest at the level of a State, except in Estonia. "The citizen is considered to be a client, an 'end user', just like in the private sector. Satisfying that client is a major objective that leads to a conceptualisation outside of public services, one that's faster and more effective,"[2] is how Kévin Chavanne, who studied in Estonia, explains it.

In 2006, the e-Governance Academy published a study, which revealed that "main efforts are not linked to technology, but to organisation, reforms of processes and the implementation of tools. The most important elements are political willingness, organisational reforms, the adaptation of legal frameworks and the revision of work processes."

It must be said that the State knows how to put itself into the mindset of a start up and that, as Arnaud Castaignet[3] notes, "it's all a different state of mind, one with less hierarchy, more young people

---

2. Interview with the authors.

3. Former Head of Public Relations for the e-Residency programme,

given important responsibilities, more accessible managers and the freedom to suggest new ideas." The golden rules of building the Estonian digital State are similar to those for start ups: transparency and the possibility of control for the citizen, researching solutions, a citizen-centred approach, resilience, small steps, the agile working method, trust and simplicity of use. We should also note here the fluidity of the State's relationship with the private sector: "More than a network between the entirety of the public administration, the Estonian platform-state is open to civil society, citizens and economic actors."[4]

Martin Kaevats, National Digital Advisor on the Information Society and Innovation to the Government Office of Estonia, sums up the process in two crucial steps[5]:"'The first stage is to build general awareness so people know what can be done with their data. The second is actual control and management of the data systems. That's why building centralised information systems is not a good idea because in today's world it's not a question of if, but when, this information will be compromised. If you spread it around, if something small happens it can be more easily managed.'

This is the principle behind X-Road, which provides the backbone to digitalisation in Estonia. 'The system allows data sharing across different authorities in a

---

4.   Antoine Picron, in his report for the Institut Sapiens.

5.   *"How Estonia nurtures a national digital identity"*,Global Intelligence for the CIO, August 2019.

secure and private way over the open internet. However, with X-Road, the point is that you should not put all your eggs in one basket. Instead, spread it around, so if one of those baskets falls or there's a cyber-attack, nothing really gets lost.'"

The technical bases of the Estonian digital State

The Estonian platform-state is often compared to an App Store, it relies on three founding principles[6]:

1. An infrastructure called X-road (crossroads), which is a system for the saving and exchanging of data that allows ministers, public agencies and private partners to share data; this ensures overall interoperability.

2. A system for digital and mobile identification (an electronic identity card or e-ID) used by more than 90% of the population, which allows for secure and authenticated access to services.

3. A level of services accessible via multiple portals (the biggest being the official State portal, eesti.ee).

X-Road, the first pillar of the platform-State, makes the interoperability of different information systems possible, particularly the distribution of personal information, so that citizens are asked for that information once in their entire lives.

---

6.   *e-Estonia: e-Governance in Practice*, e-Governance Academy, 2017.

For the user, meaning the citizen, X-Road is invisible: it's a structure for the exchange of distributed data for information systems. X-Road organises a secure exchange of personal data on the internet, between different information systems. Fundamentally, it doesn't rely on the same technology as blockchain but it works on the same philosophy: even before blockchain, it was an example of a decentralised system, and certain Estonians say that they were inspired by their isolated village communities when building this decentralised network. X-Road makes the encryption of data, interoperability and transparency possible. This system offers decentralised and user-friendly navigation between different State services (data sets).

Put more simply, X-Road could be compared to a bus that transports distributed services. At its core, the different administrations communicate between each other and exchange data by using APIs (application programming interfaces), which are similar to exchange crossroads, all of this possible without ever passing through one central point. Information is stocked in a decentralised system, so that if one administration needs it for a specific file, it must communicate with other administrations, without ever contacting you. However, as you own your data, you can follow how each civil servant is using it. Your electronic ID card allows you to connect to the platform, have access to your medical file, your taxes and your children's school, etc., all with a few clicks.

At the heart of X-Road, certified members communicate directly, without an intermediary, by using a secure peer-to-peer connection. All messages (requests and responses) are electronically signed, stamped with the date and time and sent via an encrypted channel with mutual authentication. As of October 2019, 500 million requests have been made through X-Road.

In an October 7, 2014 article entitled "The Architecture of X-Road", Andres Kütt describes the system in the following words:

"X-Road consists of three parts, technical, organisational and legal, none of which is capable of delivering its full value separate from the others.

From the technical perspective, X-Road consists of identical security servers located at organisational network boundaries and a set of centralised services. Fundamentally, the system is a peer-to-peer system, with interoperability being enforced by centrally distributed software rather than standards.

Organisationally, X-Road is a centrally funded team whose responsibility is the maintenance of central services, development of the security server software and communication with the community that runs and consumes services, using the system.

Legally, X-Road is a set of legislative acts issued by the Government of Estonia, establishing clear ownership rules around citizen-related data and stating that all government agencies using a legally significant information system must make that information system available to others using X-Road and X-Road only."

The Nordic Institute for Interoperability Solutions (NIIS), a joint institution founded by the Estonian and Finnish governments and head of the development administration for X-Road, published a full article about the worldwide abuse of the term "blockchain".[7]

The article explains that "X-Road is not based on blockchain technology – one of this year's buzzwords after the success of bitcoin and other cryptocurrencies based on its technology. Blockchain is a distributed, decentralised and public database that is updated through a consensus protocol: every node has a full copy of the database and the blocks stored in the database are linked to each other using cryptographic hash functions. X-Road is the backbone of Estonian digital society and allows the databases of the public and private sectors to exchange data. The common factor between blockchain and X-Road is that they both use cryptographic hash functions for linking data items to each other." These cryptographic hash functions existed before the invention of the two systems, which still doesn't mean that X-Road is based on blockchain technology.

Electronic signatures and authentications form the second pillar of the platform-State. These are the legal equivalent of a signature done by hand or a visual identification done in person. The e-ID system (a digital ID card) opens the door to all other e-services by guaranteeing the maximum level of security and integrity. This ID card is the only mandatory proof of identity in Estonia. The most recent statistics show that there are over 1.2 million active users

7.   *"There is no blockchain technology in the X-Road"*, NIIS, April 26, 2018.

of the ID card, meaning almost 94% of the country's 1.3 inhabitants. This makes the Estonian digital identification system the most used in the world.

Security is at the heart of the State's concerns and the aim is to prioritise the protection of personal data. Estonians use public internet, but the data is encrypted and digitally signed. Since 2007, the electronic ID card has been supplemented with a Mobile-ID that ensures electronic identification via one's mobile phone. As former President Ilves recalls: "In 2008, 2007 we put all key data on the blockchain. The main issue was data integrity. If someone publishes your bank account, you might feel annoyed. If someone changes the record of your blood type it can be fatal."[8]

In September 2017, a security breach was detected on the digital ID cards' chips. Teams of engineers immediately went to work to fix it. All of this unfolded with total transparency. In reaction to the discovery of this security breach in the Infineon chips, Prime Minister Jüri Ratas declared: "Estonia has successfully risen to the greatest challenge in its history as a digital country. The temporary vulnerability of the ID card did not have any consequences, notably legal ones, before a solution was found and the trust of the people in electronic services remains high. The success story of the e-State can only be based on cooperation,

8.   "I'm Former Estonian President Toomas Hendrik Ilves, and This is How I Work", *Lifehacker*, October 16, 2019.

in which a role of their own is played by strong IT specialists from the private sector, researchers from universities, as well as a smart State that skilfully handles their knowledge." According to him, these are the people who are critical to the resolving of a crisis. "If, alongside correcting old mistakes and keeping IT systems working, we also wish to develop them, we must invest significantly more than before and not only in systems, but also people. Competent people are the key issue of the digital society—this was definitely one of the biggest lessons from the crisis.

The third pillar of the platform-State is eesti.ee, the official e-services portal of the Estonian State, which was created in 2003, and offers secure access to all e-services offered in Estonia. This was ranked 1st by the European Commission for digital public services in 2017.[9]

The digital portal provides the user easy access, while also offering the government an effective platform to incorporate and promote new services. In 2014, esti.ee gave access to 815 e-services and had been visited by Estonians who were based in over 200 countries across the globe. In total, e-services saw over 7 million views, or five times more than the total population of Estonia. Andres Kütt from the Estonian Information System Authority, declared: "Why have we succeeded where everyone else

9.   DESI ranking, Digital Economy and Society Index, European Commission, 2017.

has failed? Because you cannot regulate everything. Instead, you must make sure that things are working and create support. At the beginning, people asked us, why are you giving us this stupid card that we have to pay for? Our response was the services that we were able to provide. One of the first decisive examples was the reimbursement of overpaid taxes, in just five hours."

This system has thousands of public services that are accessible on line: 99.5% of public services are electronic. Indrek Õnnik, former project manager of the Estonia Showroom[10], joked: "There are only three things you can't do online: get married, get divorced and buy a house." Furthermore, the "only once" principle from 1997 has become a legal imperative, so that authorities cannot ask an individual to provide information that has already been provided to any other administrative entity. The administrations themselves will go look for the necessary information, which represents a very significant time-saving measure.

What does this mean in concrete terms? Let's take the example of a child being born. Imagine not having to go to city hall to register the birth, of everything being done automatically, from accessing the health system and signing up for family allowances to registering for school. "Katariina Järvi was born on February 5, 2017 in Tartu, the second biggest city in Estonia. The maternity ward immediately transmitted news of her birth to the administration. At the register

---

10. Now Global Affairs Director in the Government's CIO Office.

of births, a file was created in her name, which generated the issuing of her digital identity. This will never disappear and will be useful to her almost every single

day. For everything, absolutely everything. This is the beginning of e-citizenship for this little girl who, like 1.3 million other Estonians, is now part of the most developed digital nation in the world..."

This is not the beginning of a science-fiction novel, but rather, the first lines of an article written by Emmanuelle Ducros, entitled *"Bienvenue en e-Estonie, le premier état réel à l'administration 100% dématérialisée"* [Welcome to e-Estonia, the First Real State with a 100% Digital Administration].[11] As Pierre Gronlier, French information engineer who worked for Skype in Estonia puts it: "We bought our first car and our first house in Estonia, our children were born in Estonia, a country where we didn't know the language or the law, and we had no problem completing actions that would have taken weeks or months in France. There's a disconcerting simplicity to it. And that's not even taking into account how a lot of private businesses use the identification service: no need to create multiple accounts and enter the same personal data over and over again to pay for gas, electricity, water, or the internet. In five years, I had to physically sign four or five pieces of paper."[12]

---

11. *L'Opinion*, June 5, 2017.
12. Interview with the authors.

Examples of online services

X-Road was built in multiple phases. Below, we've listed the steps taken to create some of the major services:

1996
Banks offer online services and, today (2017), 99.8% of banking transactions are completed electronically.

2000
Introduction of the electronic ID card or e-ID.

e-Tax

Online tax payments are now commonplace. With a secure e-ID, the taxpayer can connect to the system, confirm the entered data, make any necessary changes then finish by approving the document with a digital signature. The process takes, on average, three to five minutes and today, 98% of tax returns in Estonia are filled out electronically.

In addition to declaring individual revenue, the system also works for the following tasks:
- An enterprise's tax returns, including employee contributions.
- Value Added Tax returns.
- Excise duty returns (alcohol, tobacco, fuel, packaging, etc.).
- INF declarations.
- Customs declarations.

m-Parking

Today, 90% of paid parking is done via Mobile Parking.

e-Cabinet

The Information System for Government Sessions, better known as e-Cabinet, is used by the Estonian government to streamline its decision-making processes. It allows ministers to prepare and lead meetings, examine minutes and complete other tasks, without ever having to use paper.

At the heart of this system is a multi-user database, as well as a planner that keeps important information organised and updated in real time and gives ministers a clear overview of each item under discussion. Well before a cabinet session begins, the ministers access the system to review each agenda item and determine their position. If they have any objections or wish to speak on a certain topic, they simply click on the corresponding box. That way, the different ministers' positions are known before the cabinet session and decisions that have no objections are adopted without debate, saving considerable amounts of time. Furthermore, decisions that are made during cabinet meetings can be sent by e-mail to interested parties or posted online, even while the meeting is still going on. Estonia is always innovating, even on the political level, as Martens Kaevats explains in a recent interview[13]:"From 2000, the government became the first in the world to hold meetings [supported by] digital tech. What that has

---

13.   "How Estonianurtures a national digital identity", Global intelligence for the CIO, August 2019.

allowed us to do is reduce the length of meetings. Previously, government meetings lasted on average five hours, during which around 50 to 60 matters of state were decided. Last year, the average was 15 minutes. The shortest was in August, when we had a 22-second government meeting during which 50 decisions were made."

2002

Electronic signature

Electronic signatures help each citizen save 1 Euro per action and five days per year. It's estimated that simplifying this piece of administration represents a savings of at least 2% of the GDP. And that's not including how a stack of paper that reaches the height of the Eiffel Tower is saved every month.

2003

e-Geoportal

This geoportal is administered by the Estonian Land Board and is a practical tool that pools together information from a variety of map-based servers and spatial data services (notably, the electronic land registry was created by the Datel company) and contains information on the value, natural status and use of real estate.

Paired with the geographic information system (GIS), the e-Geoportal provides geographic data via X-Road, enabling advanced map-based visualisations that power the different location-based services available in Estonia. This is part of the Estonian Spatial Data Infrastructure, which is itself an integral part of the Infrastructure for Spatial Information in Europe (INSPIRE).

The e-Land Register is another important e-service that connects the official property database, in this way exchanging information regarding the property and limited real rights on real estate properties in Estonia. This electronic register has transformed the way property transactions are carried out in Estonia today, eliminating the need to visit public offices, and significantly reducing the time required for a real estate transaction.

A critical tool for the real estate market, it provides total transparency by listing the registered owners of each property holding, showing the property boundaries and providing other information that potential buyers need to know (cadastral information, charges, mortgage information, etc.). Finally, both businesses and individual citizens benefit from this practical access to land registry information and from the possibility of being able to confirm information about their properties, in just a few clicks.

e-Law

Since February 2003, this service, formally known as the "Electronic Coordination System for Draft Legislation" allows the public to read every draft law submitted. Users can see who submitted the legislation, its current status and changes made to it as it passes through the parliamentary process. Once an act becomes a law, it's published in the official online state gazette, *RiigiTeataja*, another searchable database that acts as an open legal library.

A similar system is used by Tallinn City Council. It makes it possible to follow all council sessions online, while city legislation and other documents are available on the municipal homepage.

2005

i-Voting

In 2005, Estonia became the first country in the world to introduce online voting. The 2019 parliamentary elections yielded 247,232 electronic votes out of a total of 565,028 votes, a 40% increase from the 186,034 i-Votes of the previous election. According to initial reports, 43.75% of all votes were cast online, a new i-Voting record. For comparison, 31.7% of the votes in the 2017 local elections were i-Votes.[14]

Estonians like to clarify that i-Voting is completely unrelated to the electronic voting systems used elsewhere, which they see as mere gadgets. With i-Voting, you can vote from the comfort of your bed, from the other end of the world on your computer or with your mobile phone.

Geoffroy Berson, ex-Attaché for Digital Innovation Cooperation at the Institut Français in Estonia[15]remembers: "At university, everyone was

---

14. e-estonia
15. Now digital ambassador GIZ in Madagascar.

shocked to see our fellow Estonian students voting on their mobiles in between classes."[16]

2007

e-Business

The e-Business Register is an online platform that's linked to an official database that compiles in real time the data related to legal business entities in Estonia. It also houses the Company Registration Portal (CRP), an internet platform that allows entrepreneurs to submit requests, documents and annual reports to the e-Business Register. These can only be signed with an ID-Card or a Mobile-ID.

Thanks to this digital system, Estonia has significantly reduced its administrative operating costs and has increased its attractiveness to foreign investors, who can now set up their businesses in 18 minutes (as opposed to the five days that the traditional method would have required). The following are available services through the Company Registration Portal:

• Create a new company or NGO and submit the forms for changing, selling or eliminating the registration data.

• An e-Platform to compile, sign and submit annual reports.

• E-billing, an online accounting software that helps start ups and small businesses keep their accounts in order.

---

16. Interview with the authors.

e-Health Record

The Estonian online healthcare system is among the most ambitious of its kind, and serves as an example of why this small EU country is considered one of the most advanced digital nations in the world.

"The more extensive and systematic implementation of online health solutions will allow us to achieve economies of scale, have a more flexible service, improve people's health by demonstrating greater efficiency, taking preventative measures and saving billions of Euros," declared Toomas Hendrik Ilves, then president of Estonia, during the launch of this service.

The electronic health file (e-Health Record) is a nationwide system that integrates data from Estonia's different healthcare providers to create a common record that every patient, as the owner of his or her personal data, can access online. Doctors are required by law to transmit data to this online health record. This record consolidates all relevant health data for each patient, including recent appointments, analyses and diagnoses, as well as time-critical information like allergies, prescriptions, etc.

Functioning very much like a centralised, national database, the e-Health Record retrieves data as necessary from various providers, who may be using different systems, and presents it in a standard format via the e-Patient portal. This is a powerful tool for doctors because it allows them to easily access a patient's records from a single electronic file. Doctors can read test results as they are transmitted by laboratories, including image files like X-rays, even from remote hospitals.

There are over 20 million health documents (case summaries, vaccinations, dental information, medical X-Rays, etc.) in the e-Health system. More than 95% of the data produced by hospitals and doctors have been digitised and citizens can easily find their medical files and prescriptions, as well as locate the health professional that is best-suited to their particular case.

Madis Tiik, a doctor and public health expert for a number of institutions, presents the next step, Healthcare 4.0, as the future solution for Estonia. He describes, with just a few words, what the future of health could look like. First of all, empowerment: people will be more aware of the factors that influence their health and each person will gradually become more responsible for the management of their health. Secondly, mobility: patients will be able to access information wherever they happen to be, at any time of their choosing. In the future, Estonia will provide point-of-care devices—equipment that patients can use themselves. Finally, Estonia will provide global health accounts and introduce the benefits of artificial intelligence-based health methods.

For Estonia's Minister of Health and Labour, Riina Sikkut[17]: "...another digital solution we are quite proud of is our drug interaction and counter indication decision support software. This software is connected to our e-prescription database, so whenever a doctor tries to prescribe something that might

---

17. "Learning from the Estonian e-health system", Health Europa, Janurary 2019.

interact with one of the medicines a patient is taking, they get a warning from the system. This helps avoid unnecessary side effects or adverse events related to medications. We have estimated that around 15-17% of prescriptions get changed after these warnings are displayed."

2010

e-Prescription

Digital prescriptions are considered to be the most popular of the e-services offered to the population. 95% of medication is purchased via an electronic prescription.

The digital prescription Service is a centralised and paperless system that electronically delivers medical prescriptions, via an online form. In Estonia, all hospitals and pharmacies are connected to the system.

At the pharmacy, all a patient needs to do is present an ID card. The pharmacist then retrieves the patient's information, finds their prescription online and issues the medication. The system draws on data from the national health insurance fund, so that it directly applies any state medical subsidies and discounts that the patient is entitled to. Another major advantage of the system is that doctor visits are no longer needed for repeat prescriptions. Patients can contact their doctors by e-mail, Skype or phone and the doctors can issue repeat prescriptions with just a few clicks. This saves time for patients and doctors and reduces the administrative strain on hospitals.

2014
Driving licenses and vehicle registrations.

2015

e-Ambulance
Electronic ambulances are plugged into X-Road, so that ambulance drivers can have direct access to patients' medical files. This means that the team which arrives when you have chest pains can access your latest cardiology report, as well as all of your physiological parameters (blood type, pulse, arterial tension, temperature, etc.). With the e-Ambulance service, ambulance drivers can also pre-register a patient while en route to the hospital so that the necessary tests, treatments and surgeries will be ready once they arrive.

e-Court
The electronic Court is a complete system for managing legal proceedings.

The initial complaint is entered via a digital public portal that's open 24/7. In the next hour, the court clerk confirms the case and chooses the first audience. The appointed judge will receive all the necessary information, while they and other participants can electronically submit evidence, respond to questions and even have legal representatives and lawyers engage in the process.

If the case is a simple one, the hearing will be held electronically, without it being necessary to go to court. All participants will receive the decision via the public portal, using X-road technologies. The concluding and court bailiff proceedings are also digitised: fines are received automatically, without you needing to take care of payments in person.

A *New Yorker* article highlights the benefits of the e-Court: "In Tallinn's courtrooms, judges' benches are fitted with two monitors, for consulting information during the proceedings, and case files are assembled according to the once-only principle. The police make reports directly into the system; forensic specialists at the scene or in the lab do likewise. Lawyers log on—as do judges, prison wardens, plaintiffs, and defendants, each through his or her portal. The Estonian courts used to be notoriously backlogged, but that is no longer the case."[18]

"'No one was able to say whether we should increase the number of courts or increase the number of judges,' says Timo Mitt, a manager at Netgroup, which the government hired to build the architecture. Digitising both streamlined the process and helped identify points of delay. Instead of setting up prisoner transport to trial—fraught with security risks—Estonian courts can teleconference defendants into the courtroom from prison."

Coming soon

e-Death

In order to console the loved ones of the deceased, Industry 62 and the government are currently working

---

18. "Estonia the digital republic", *The New Yorker*, December 18, 2017.

on a project that should be available soon. Their goal is to eliminate the administrative steps taken after the passing of a loved one, with less paperwork and more streamlining of how death certificates are dealt with in the public registry.

Imagine not having to inform each administrative body about a death. Instead, the doctor will issue a death certificate, and that will be enough to ensure that all administrations and businesses connected to X-Road know of the situation.

Reporting 3.0

The objective of Reporting 3.0 is to reduce the burden on entrepreneurs when it comes to the mandatory submitting of data to public institutions. The first step of the project is to simplify the process so that declaring salaries and labour force spending is made automatic. A new portal for the tax and customs administrations will be completed in 2020, where the exchange of information between businesses and tax authorities will be automatic and will only require access to the necessary data. This service will help save time and money, so that businesses can focus on their development and people can be more productive at work.

Coping with AI

AI is one of the main themes of the government roadmap. Siim Sikkut, the Government CIO of Estonia explains[19]:"We are trying to catch up on using artificial

---

19. "Building the Digital Government – Estonia's Digital Transformation", Under the Hood, October 26, 2019.

intelligence and data science in the public sector. This includes using machine learning and existing narrow artificial intelligence applications for better decision-making and the automation of services as well. We are moving forward with the first set of trials with this technology. There are some low-hanging fruits such as image recognition. In a policy agency, we have a few people who are looking at speeding cameras and identifying numbers on plates. That is a readily available algorithm out there in the market, so we don't need to invent or use resources in creating it. There are many low-hanging fruits that we will start with and with all the examples we will build up an appetite for change among the agencies. We need to demonstrate to agencies what can be done, what the benefits of products in the market are, and begin using them. It's not rocket science, but concrete practical IT projects with immediate beneficial outcomes."

Estonia's goal is create an environment where the government anticipates the services that citizens need, before they request them.

"'Blockchain can help make this project a reality'", explains Estonian president Kersti Kaljuliad. "'The government is currently piloting a blockchain application related to traffic accident reporting. Once an accident is reported and registered online, the parties involved would be provided information on how the resolution of the case and the insurance outcome are moving forward. The entire case could be handled in 30 minutes...'"[20]

20. "Estonia experiments with blockchain, smart services and 'data embassies'", *GCN*, April 4, 2018.

Implementation

The digital Estonian State wasn't built in a day. It accepted the fact that it would have to proceed slowly, adding services one by one and knowing that if something didn't work right away, it wasn't the end of the world. What was important was the infrastructure and access cards for unique authentication purposes: adding more services was simple.

This approach is in sharp contrast to that of more established States, which want to complete large-scale infrastructure projects. Estonians know how to recognise their errors and change the system accordingly, a fact that Kadi Metsandi emphasises: "That's what happened at the beginning with the computerisation of schools, which didn't work well. We have a very fast-moving capacity for resilience."[21]

"'Estonia has also failed several times,'" recounts Siim Sikkut, the Estonian government's CIO. "'But we failed fast and on a smaller scale.'" Last year, the Estonian government wrote off a new social welfare system that, according to Sikkut, was going in the wrong direction. "'Don't make us into a wonderland! Quite clearly, it's very hard to keep digital capacity at the same level in many different institutional agencies. In Estonia, we've made quite an effort to improve skills and training and raise the awareness of the people in government about what digital is and how to be agile and user-centric. Generally speaking, these

---

21. Former Economic counsellor to the Estonian Embassy in Paris. Now Director of Development Cooperation and Humanitarian Aid at Estonian Foreign Ministry
Interview with the authors.

trainings are aimed at engineers, so the trick is to aim these efforts and trainings at the politicians or civil servants who aren't techies at all.'"

"'At the end of the day, a successful transformation doesn't rely on the technology introduced but rather, on the transformation of the process.'"[22]

Even today, not every single service works well. As the political science researcher Kadi Maria Vooglaid notes, everything isn't perfect. A notable example is e-Health: electronic prescriptions are working well, but the service isn't yielding the expected beneficial effects regarding medical files, including better coordination between professionals, between hospitals and general practitioners and fewer redundant medical treatments.

Another failure: the government's platform for consultations, which hasn't brought about a surge of democratic participation.

What about data security and cybersecurity?

Some people see in the interconnected Estonian system the very high possibility for threats against individual freedoms. It's completely the opposite! Transparency reigns supreme on the eesti.ee platform. Here, you can consult your profile in real time so that you always know which departments are exchanging your data.

---

22. "Creating a digital society: Can Australia learn something from Estonia?", cio.com, February 17, 2018.

Don't understand why the Tallinn city hall needs information about your personal records? In just one click, you can put in a request for additional information. Not convinced by the department's explanations? One more click and you can file a complaint. Fewer than 700 complaints were filed in 2017, but this option is an extremely valuable one, as it guarantees the citizens' trust in the system. In France, do we know exactly what the law authorises when it comes to the exchanging of data between administrative departments? We don't know and we can't see it, which means that we can't protest it. However, there's no obligation for this exchange to be done for us. This is what the Estonian president highlights in an interview that appeared in *L'Obs*[23]: we know much less about which pieces of our information are being exchanged by the administration than Estonians do. Furthermore, they understood the importance of creating a positive feedback loop around citizens, who always know why their data is being exchanged.

Additionally, as former President Ilves explained in an interview with *The Guardian*[24], there's another important element that's even more pertinent than respecting privacy: data integrity. We're very preoccupied with who can find out about our blood type and not so much with who might be able to modify this information, and how. The Estonian doctrine regarding cybersecurity focuses on this question of integrity, in technical and legal terms.

23. "Estonie : Bienvenue au e-Paradis" [Estonia: Welcome to e-Paradise], Dominique Nora, *L'Obs*, September 29, 2017.

24. "E-stonia: the country using tech to rebrand itself as the anti-Russia", *The Guardian*, April 21, 2016.

In a Tweet on April 4, 2018, Adam Rang, ex-Chief evangelist for the e-Residency programme[25], expressed his point of view on this question very clearly: "I'm often asked why Estonians, as part of a digital nation, have so much trust in their government. I've explained that we're just as cynical as everyone else. Maybe even more so. But our digital identities help us hold the government responsible and take control of our data. We trust ourselves." The Eurobarometer survey published in November 2017 reveals that 59% of Estonians trust their government, while the average in the EU is 35%.

The threat of cyberattacks is also taken very seriously by Estonia, which was the victim of a major attack in 2007, in all likelihood launched by Russia. Internet providers came under attack, as did all government sites, e-mail systems, online banking systems and other online services. The country resisted without significant damage, proof of the robustness of Estonian cyberspace. Following this attack, in 2008 Estonia welcomed the NATO Cooperative Cyber Defence Centre of Excellence (CCDCOE), whose headquarters are in Tallinn. Theinternational military organisation aims to enhance capability, cooperation and information sharing among NATO member nations and partners in cyber defence, and the centre brings together researchers, analysts and educators from the military, government, academia and industry. This is accomplished through education, research and development, as well as the sharing of consultation processes and lessons learned.

25. Now an Estonian sauna exporter.

In May 2019, nine countries signed on to joining the CCDCOE: Japan, Switzerland, Croatia, Montenegro and Slovenia have already started the accession process, while Luxembourg, Canada, Australia and the Republic of Ireland have announced their intention to join. "In the field of cyber security, countries' perceptions of the gravity of the situation have changed dramatically over the last two or three years," said Col. Jaak Tarien, head of the CCDCOE,[26] which as of summer 2019, had a reported membership of 25 countries.

In 2017, the government launched a global first by deciding to open an e-Embassy in Luxembourg, which would back up all of the country's data, while enjoying the same diplomatic immunity as any other embassy. This data centre acts as a total back up tool that protects all of the country's data and which will allow the State to continue functioning, in the case of any attack, cyber or land-based. A few months later, the Principality of Monaco decided to follow Estonia's example and also open an e-Embassy in Luxembourg.[27]

In the wake of this world premiere, Estonia maintains cybersecurity as its top priority and as a result, has become an invaluable global pioneer in best practices for a safe cyberspace. On September 12, 2019, the Ministry of Foreign Affairs was equipped with a new cyber-diplomacy department.

---

26. "Nine more nations join NATO cyberdefensecenter", ERR, May 10 2019.

27. « Monaco l'autre Estonie du Luxembourg » [Monaco, the other Estonia in Luxembourg], *Paperjam*, May 10, 2019.

Cyber-diplomacy primarily refers to the behaviour of States within cyberspace, as well as their compliance with cyber-norms, confidence-building measures and existing international law. Multiple forms of cooperation have been established within this realm, in the UN, the EU, the OSCE, NATO, the Council of Europe, the OECD and other international organisations with which Estonia shares its field expertise.

This new cyber-diplomacy department falls within the scope of the Minister of Foreign Affairs. It will be led by Heli Tiirmaa-Klaarl, Estonia's ambassador-at-large for cybersecurity. The creation of this new department coincides with Estonia's election to the position of a non-permanent member of the UN Security Council. Estonia will begin its membership in 2020 and will hold its seat for the next two years, along with four other new non-permanent members: Niger, Tunisia, Vietnam and Saint Vincent and the Grenadines.

As Anett Numa, speaker at the e-Estonia briefing centre wrote in an article last September[28]: "In Estonia, cybersecurity means fully protecting the digital society and the way of life as a whole. Many visiting delegations frequently question whether attacks on public sector digital services happen often. In fact, the answer is clear – attacks happen daily and everywhere. Last year, the number of attacks to the systems in Estonia rose to 17,440. However, the number of critical incidents has decreased [by] 37% comparing to the previous two years. The main purpose of the cyber

---

28. "Cyber threats no longer know national borders", e-estonia, September 2019.

defence policyis to help ensure people's trust in the information society and avoid the loss of data. (...) Estonia has opened CR14 Cyber Security Exercises and Training Centre under the Ministry of Defence. It is crystal clear that protecting a digital state requires also Cyber Forces."

A unique relationship between public and private

X-Road incorporates the know-how of private companies like Cybernetica, Helmes, GuardTime, Nortal and Datel. (Cybernetica came out of Tallinn University before being turned into a private company.)

The main banks (Hansapank and Ühispank, today Swedbank and SEB) played a central role in the development of the first electronic solutions and contributed to the popularity of online services in Estonia, by providing very high-quality online banking services. By offering free ID-card readers and encouraging their clients to use their ID-cards, in order to make their transactions secure, banks helped promote more frequent use of them and more widespread application of the national electronic identification document. These examples showcase the narrowness of public-private relationships.

From the 3,195 different services that are available, thanks to X-Road, nearly half are outside of the public sphere. They function in the same way as public services for citizens who can use their e-IDs and transmit data. This is the case, for example, with parking lots and banks, but also large water, electricity, gas and telecommunications companies. Sometimes, there's even a public service managed by the private sector, as is the case for e-Ambulance and Industry62, the company that also developed interoperability and data exchange solutions between Finland and Estonia.

There exists a real desire to improve the services offered by the State by turning to solutions that have been developed by start ups, when that's possible. The Parliament does not hesitate to quickly change laws in order to allow for new innovations.

Ex-Prime Minister of Estonia, Taavi Roivas, summarises this approach: "We made a very conscious choice to build shared platforms with X-Road and joint digital identity, rather than allow diverse development. The idea was also to put in place the right conditions so that digital innovation can flourish in all parts of the public sector and society, bottom-up. If some area falls behind, we try to lead by example and kick-start things top-down too."[29]

To help speed up innovation, the State tendered building and securing the digital signature-certificate systems to private parties, namely a consortium led by local banks and telecommunication companies.

The digitisation of the social security system provides two examples of the way in which the State and the private sector work together.

---

29. *Government as a platform*, Marggetts&Naumann.

The cooperation between Nortal—one of the biggest ICT companies—and the Estonian Unemployment and Insurance Fund (EUIF) for the automation of the distribution of social assistance grants is a clear example of how the State can better respond to the needs of its citizens, by way of digitisation.

Between the second trimester of 2008 and the first trimester of 2010, the unemployment rate had risen spectacularly in Estonia, reaching a record 19.5%. Today, (in 2017), after the first phase of slow reduction, the rate has increased by 5.3%. In 2011, with more than 14%[30] of the Estonian labour force potentially needing unemployment insurance and connected services, the Estonian Unemployment Insurance Fund seemed to be on the verge of a crisis within a crisis. Nortal rose to the challenge of automating the process of evaluating eligibility for unemployment services and disability allowances. In the last few years, the company has developed and fully implemented two different platforms, TETRIS for disabilities and EMPIS for unemployment, which have significantly reduced the workload of the fund's civil servants.

Notably, this has involved fewer items being requested, thanks to the connection with X-Road, but also to an improved eligibility evaluation process, especially in light of the 2016 working ability reform. With a maximum of 30 days (according to the law) to complete the evaluation process, any system delays or defects directly impact the quality of life for those involved.

---

30. Official figures from the Estonian Ministry of Employment.

TETRIS has made the reform's objectives more easily accessible, allowing the fund to collect data from 13 different databases and to encourage the reintegration of disabled people into the labour market.

The advantages of the implementations of EMPIS and TETRIS, from a public administration point of view, are considerable:

- The time required to sign up for the EUIF as an unemployed person has gone from one hour to 10 minutes.
- The funding granted by EMPIS for the starting of a company has allowed for the creation of 1,292 new companies in two and a half years, which has generated additional revenue of 6.4 million Euros in VAT every year.
- The matching of job offers to job-seekers is automatic.
- The verification of data in order to avoid fraud and to ensure that a person is eligible for the services and benefits of unemployment insurance.
- 90% of the cases where work capacity is being evaluated are completed one week before the cut-off date.
- The movement from manual to electronic handling of requests makes it so that one person can treat as many cases as 100 civil servants working full time could have before. In five years, 15,000 people with disabilities could find jobs that were suitable for them, representing an overall increase of about 143 million Euros in tax revenue.

Here's a second example and another project: Nortal is going to build a new system for the Estonian Social Insurance Board which will involve about 700,000 people per month and will distribute over 20% of the country's annual budget per year. The system will handle over 2 billion Euros in pensions and benefits every year; it will be one of the most complicated large-scale digital projects in Estonia for the next two years.

Over the course of the project, the internal processes of the Estonian Social Insurance Board will be reworked and its services will be remodelled according to the needs of the final users: the technology is thus a lever for a much larger public transformation.

Egon Veermäe, Director of the Estonian Social Insurance Board, is also saying that it's important for the Board's services to be developed in a comprehensible and easily accessible manner, without the need for submitted requests. This is a fundamental point when trying to understand the Estonian model: the process of improving the relationship with citizens is constant.

All of these technological innovations shouldn't make us forget the meaning of the Estonian model. The report from the American NGO Freedom House, entitled "Freedom on the Net 2015" called Estonia one of the best connected countries in the world where internet access and citizen support for online services have become widespread. For Estonian president Kersti Kaljul, "the electronic signature is an inclusive step which increases social cohesion". Something to consider for those of us who still think of the digital in terms of fractures and not social inclusion... The Estonian model also corresponds to a new social approach for digital technology. And as Xavier Schneider, a French e-Health entrepreneur who is familiar with Estonia, notes, what if Estonia is a Digital Nation that relies more on humans than technology?

5. FROM START UP NATION TO A NATION WITHOUT BORDERS

The economy, in a nutshell

The numbers speak for themselves: GDP (gross domestic product) per inhabitant of Estonia went from $100 in 1991 to $22,927 in 2018![1]

Starting in June 1992, the kroon was Estonia's official currency, with an exchange rate that was fixed to the German mark (1 mark = 8 kroons). After the creation of the Euro, the kroon was tied to the Euro (with an exchange rate of 1 Euro = 15.6466 kroons). In 2011, Estonia joined the eurozone and the Euro became the national currency.[2]

Between 2000 and 2008, the Estonian economy saw an average annual rise of 7%, which made Estonia one of the three EU countries with the greatest growth. During this period, the standard of living

---

1.   World bank.
2.   Estonica.org.

also improved considerably: GDP per inhabitant went from 45% of the EU's average in 2000 to 67% of that average in 2008.

The economic situation changed in the spring of 2007. Banks cut the number of loans they were granting, consumer trust plummeted and the real estate market went into decline. While the rapid growth in income continued, by the beginning of 2008 private consumption was falling, as were investments in the private sector. In the fall of 2008, at the height of its economic crisis, Estonia saw the quick collapse of its exports, a loss of cash flow and a slump in consumer and company confidence. Estonia even reported a 14.7% drop in GDP by 2009.

Economic growth was on the rise once more in the second trimester of 2010 and annual GDP rose by 2.5%, when compared to the previous year. In 2016, according to Statistics Estonia, annual GDP rose by 1.7%[3] and Estonian economic growth held steady at around 3% from 2017 to 2018.

The Estonian economy is highly dependent on that of its neighbours. Its main commercial partners are Finland, Sweden, Latvia and Germany, and in 2016, 78% of Estonia's overall trade was done with EU member countries.

The recovery has led to a decline in unemployment: the annual average unemployment rate, which at its highest during the economic crisis had reached 19%, fell back down to 6.8% in 2016 and 5.3% in 2017.

There was also an increase in the average monthly salary, which had risen to €1,146 in 2016 (marking a

---

3.   GDP of Estonia: 23.14 billion USD (2016), World Bank.

2.5% increase since €1,065 in 2015). Despite the crisis, Estonian public finances remain very healthy: the budget deficit sits at 0.6% and public debt represents only 9.5% of GDP, an amount more than covered by the country's reserves.[4]

According to Statistics Estonia, Estonia's GDP was worth 30.28 billion US dollars in 2018, representing a 3.9% increase since 2017. For the third consecutive year, economic growth in Estonia was more than 3%.

The gap in GDP per capita when compared to the upper half of OECD countries remains significant, although it has been narrowing steadily since the global financial crisis, thanks to increased employment and labour productivity growth. Income inequality, which is around the OECD average, has moderately decreased in recent years. Greenhouse gas emissions per capita are high and haven't dropped over the last two decades. Some of the concerns around skill shortages and high structural unemployment have been addressed, notably by boosting vocational education, encouraging the recipients of disability benefits to return to work and reducing the labour tax wedge on low-income earners. Productivity could be further accelerated by improving research collaboration between domestic and foreign institutions, strengthening infrastructure (especially by expanding access to European transport networks), and cutting down corporate insolvency procedures.

---

4. Official Estonian statistics.

Continued reinforcement of vocational education and training could boost the productivity of low wage workers, thereby making growth more inclusive, while incentives for greener buildings and a smart electric grid could help improve energy efficiency, as it has in the advanced OECD countries.[5]

Estonia, which has been a member of the EU since 2004 and the Eurozone since 2011, has a modern market-based economy and one of the higher per capita income levels in Central Europe and the Baltic region. However, its economy is highly dependent on trade, leaving it vulnerable to external shocks. Estonia's successive governments have pursued a free market, pro-business economic agenda, and adopted sound fiscal policies that have resulted in balanced budgets and the lowest debt-to-GDP ratio in the EU.

Estonia's economy benefits from robust electronics and telecommunications sectors and strong trade ties with Finland, Sweden, Germany, and Russia. The economy's 4.9% GDP growth in 2017 was the fastest it has been in the past six years, leaving the Estonian economy in the best position it has held since the financial crisis 10 years ago. In 2017, for the first time in many years, labour productivity rose faster than labour costs. Inflation also rose in 2017 to 3.5%, alongside increased global prices for food and energy, which make up a large part of Estonia's consumption.

As of now, Estonia faces two critical economic challenges: a shortage of labour, both skilled and unskilled,

---

5.   OECD

and wage growth that outpaces productivity gains. The government is currently pursuing efforts to boost productivity growth with a focus on innovations that prioritise technology startups and e-commerce.[6]

This growth model is based on the export of goods and services (€12 billion in goods, €6 billion in services). EU funding represents 9.1% of the State's budget, 3.2% of Estonia's GDP and 18.2% of public investment.

According to Coface (*Compagnie Française d'Assurance pour le Commerce Extérieur*), when it comes to trade, the Estonian economy benefits from several assets: a surplus in public accounts and low debt; close financial, trading and cultural links with Scandinavian countries; an almost total energy self-sufficiency, thanks to its oil shale resources; the development of high value-added industries (electronics, IT services, etc.) and a very favourable business environment; the digitisation of administrative features; and a flexible economic policy. The country's economic potential has it poised to quickly meet the EU average, aided especially by its low energy dependence (9%, as opposed to 54% for the EU).

Estonia's weaknesses come from it having a small, open economy that is sensitive to external shocks; a declining labour force; a shortage of skilled labour; a lack of land connections with the rest of the EU; income inequalities; and persistent poverty, especially in the predominantly Russian-speaking eastern areas of the country.

---

6. Theodora.com, February 2019.

Economic sectors

Primary sector

As a result of the economic and property reforms of the early 1990s, Estonian collective and state farms gave way to small farms and associations. The transitional period of the 1990s proved to be a difficult time for agriculture: competition with cheap imported products became an issue, and while enterprises needed new equipment and vehicles, money was nowhere to be found. In the late 1990s, it became impossible to export into Russia due to its internal crises, although it had been the principal sales outlet for Estonian agricultural produce during the Soviet occupation. Estonian agriculture benefited from the country's joining the European Union: with no customs or import restrictions, it was possible to sell food products to other European countries, and the Russian market soon opened up again, too. Estonian farmers began receiving various grants that remain significantly smaller than those in Western Europe, although manufacturing costs have risen to almost the same level. Recent years have seen the expansion of Estonian agricultural enterprises, as modern technology is used more and more.

The main farm animals raised in Estonia are milk cattle, pigs and poultry. The agricultural subsidies granted by the European Union and the Estonian government have enabled the creation of dairy production facilities that are among the most modern in the world. The average size of the Estonian bovine population is the second highest in Europe. The genetics of the cows, as well as the microchips implanted in them, greatly contribute to the very high profitability of dairy products. In fact, the average milk production per cow is more than 93,000 kilos per year, putting Estonia in second place in Europe, just after Denmark. In this regards, milk is often called Estonia's white gold.Field crops include grain crops, potatoes and vegetables. Plant products are mostly for internal use, while a considerable amount of meat is imported. Some dairy products and other specific products – e.g. cultivated and wild berries, mushrooms, ecologically pure produce, etc. -are also for export. Estonia produces far less in terms of agriculture than many other countries that are better climatically situated, but its local produce contains considerably fewer chemicals and organic farming is also gaining in popularity.

The forest is one of Estonia's most important natural resources and the source of a significant amount of its raw material. Although forestry employs just 1% of Estonia's labour force and accounts for a little over 1% of Estonia's production, it provides raw material for the timber, paper and furniture industries, which make up another 6% of overall production and which employ more than 4.5% of the workforce, making Estonia the primary European exporter of wooden houses.Agriculture represents 3% of Estonia's GDP and employs less than 4% of the labour force. Estonia is rich in oil shale, which accounts for a very large part of its energy production (80%), and which allows it to be self-sufficient in the production of electricity.

Secondary sector

The industrial sector represents 27%of Estonia's GDP and employs over 30% of the Estonian labour force. The main industries of Estonia are agri-food (dairy products and meat preparation), which accounts for over 15% of manufacturing, electronics and information technologies, the chemical industry and the wood-processing industry (wood-processing represents more than 20% of manufacturing).The industrial sector in Estonia also handles the production of textiles, machinery, equipment, electronics and oil shale energy. Estonia produces almost all of its electricity itself, using locally mined oil shale: in fact, Estonia's oil shale industry is among the most developed in the world, providing 80% of the world's oil shale.

Shipbuilding is also a significant Estonian industry. The companies in the shipbuilding sector engage in the manufacture of boats and ships, which are used for both recreational and commercial purposes. In 2015, the total turnover for commercial shipbuilding companies was £29.9 million.[7]

The metal industry plays a key role in several fields, including the manufacture and construction of machinery and equipment. It employs over 14,000 people, making it one of the largest industries after the timber and food industries and involves more than 1,300 companies.

Industry 4.0

"Industry and IT are no longer separate and discrete sectors from one another. 'Just as the educational

---

7.   "What Are The Biggest Industries In Estonia?",World Atlas, July2, 2019.

landscape is moving in the direction of interdisciplinary learning (ICT and economics in every field of study), industrial sectors are interlinked with ICT,' says Anneli Heinsoo."[8]Estonia has a sizeable Advanced Industrial sector and world-class IT expertise in areas like high tech systems, control technologies and cyber security. Supported by a collaborative ecosystem well suited to research and development, Estonia is emerging as a centre of excellence in industrial automation.[9]

Third sector
The service sector is the most developed in the country (especially transport and logistics, as well as biotechnology and financial services), representing 70% of GDP and employing around 66% of the labour force. This sector includes wholesale and retail trade; motor vehicle and motorcycle repair; transportation and storage; accommodation and food service activities; information and communication; financial and insurance activities; real estate activities; professional, scientific and technical activities; administrative and support service activities; public administration and defence; compulsory social security; education; human health and social work activities; and arts, entertainment and recreation.

Information and communications technology (ICT) is the highest performing industry. Digital alone represents 7% of Estonia's GDP, over 4,000 of its

---

8. *Life in Estonia*, March, 2016.
9. investinestonia.com, 2019.

companies and involves a €330 million investment in capital risk. The digital sector is Estonia's main asset, so we'll take some time to explore it.

From e-government to the Estonian Valley

Tallinn has become the start up centre of the world. "It's incredible: over the last few years, there has been a start up explosion. It almost feels like start ups have taken over the city. There have been multiple references now to Tallinn being the Silicon Valley of Europe," remarks Norris Koppel[10], co-founder and CEO of Monese, the application that was launched in September 2015 as the first 100% mobile current account in the United Kingdom, and which today makes over half a billion pounds sterling in transactions.

Estonia is ranked first in Europe in innovation investment, at $60 per inhabitant (that number is 33 for France and 185 for the United States)[11]. The country boasts one of the largest numbers of start ups per inhabitant in Europe: 31 start ups for every 100,000 inhabitants. In France, we have 8 start ups for every 100,000 inhabitants.[12] "Estonians make more start ups than babies," jokes Rainer Selvet, co-founder of the start up Wolf 3D.

What role have public authorities played in the start up boom? The digitisation of public services

---

10. "How Tallinn's tech talent transformed its start-up ecosystem on Thursday", *elite business*, January 18, 2018.

11. OECD.

12. Funderbeam.

appealed to the private sector, but the creation of innovative businesses also got a boost from the completely simplified administrative framework and a tax system that encouraged the reinvestment of profits.

Accordingly, the World Bank ranked Estonia 12[th]out of 190 countries in its report on where it was easiest to start a business, *Doing Business 2017*(France was 31st). The OECD named Estonia, along with Singapore and Korea, one of the countries in the world whose government is the most favourable to start ups. And MEDEF (the French Business Confederation), in its 2017 *Guide des ecosystèmes numériques mondiaux* (Guide to Digital Ecosystems Across the Globe), placed Estonia next to Israel, Singapore and the United States, as being a country which has not only built a high-performing ecosystem but also possesses a clear vision and strategy for digital technology in the next 20 years.

Estonia is paradise for those who want to start a business: the applicable statutes fit on a single page, you can manage bank accounts remotely and you can delegate any legal proceedings to others. "'The user experience of the country is really easy: setting up a business takes ten minutes online from a café,'" explains Karoli Hindriks, CEO of Jobbatical, the talent-matching platform for international tech jobs. "'You waste so much less time on things, which means you can actually invest that time in building your business.'"[13]

---

13. "How Tallinn's tech talent transformed its start-up ecosystem on Thursday", *elite business*, January 18, 2018.

Annual reports can be written online using a standardised and simplified form. "Coming from France, it's really relaxing," says Thomas Padovani. Originally from Lyon, this just-turned-30-year-old, who started with the team that founded Rentabiliweb, has made a local name for himself with the creation of AdCash. Seven years after its launch, his company, which monetises online advertising spaces, has achieved a turnover of €50 million, half of which comes from the United States, and employs about a hundred people across the globe, helping him earn the title of Entrepreneur of the Year in Estonia in 2013.[14]

For Sten Tamkivi, former head of Skype in Estonia and founder of Teleport: "You can view the country of Estonia itself as a start up: generally, the society or culture here has very little hierarchy. It's very small and nimble and that sort of environment is very positive for entrepreneurship."[15]

The local start up community also enjoys a good relationship with the government, which remains attentive and does its best to be sensitive to the needs of entrepreneurs and start ups. Sten Tamkivi explains, "One of the best things about Estonia for an entrepreneur is the speed with which decisions are made. Two years ago, I wrote an article about the things that discouraged start up creators from starting their businesses in Estonia. Within the year, those problems were dealt with, through a set of legislative changes

14. « Bienvenue en Estonie » [Welcome to Estonia], *Enjeux les Echos*, October 12, 2014. The title of Entrepreneur of the Year in Estonia is given by the firm EY Estonia.

15. "How Estonia has avoided EU's economic problems", Charlotte Ashton, BBC news, October 6, 2011.

that were passed by Parliament. You can't see such agility within governance anywhere else in the world!"

If a start up needs a law to change in order for it to keep developing, the Estonian government and Parliament are in a position to make it happen in within three months. This is what happened in July 2017, with the kilometre-long test run of the first self-driving bus in Tallinn. Starship Technologies' self-driving robotic delivery vehicle already has a law that lets it drive in the streets, thus anticipating the first accident between a robot and a car!

When listing the factors that have encouraged development in this new Tech Valley, we can't forget about Skype: the first big Estonian success and the most famous on an international scale, even if other unicorns like Bolt are making a name for themselves now.

In 2003, Niklas Zennström and Janus Friis, from Sweden and Denmark respectively, created Skype, along with Estonians Priit Kasesalu, Ahti Heinla and Jaan Tallinn. By the late 1980s, these three Estonian developers were already designing computer games. In 1989 (before Estonian independence), they had even become the first Estonians to sell a game abroad: *Cosmonaute* was purchased by a Swedish buyer for $5,000. In the early 2000s, the team continued its collaboration, perfecting its skills and developing new ideas, while working for the Swedish telecommunications company Tele2 and creating Kazaa, an application for the peer-to-peer[16] sharing of files,

---

16. Peer-to-peer, or P2P (both terms mean the same thing) refers to a peer data network between computers that distributes and receives data or

which was used to exchange MP3 music files and other files, including videos, applications and internet documents.

Kazaa popularised peer-to-peer downloading but it was sold after a series of legal setbacks involving the music and cinema industries. Looking for new ideas, the team had its eureka moment when its members realised that they could use this peer-to-peer technology to create an "internet telephone". This is how Skype was born in Tallinn. With its creation, users could speak with each other using a microphone, or enjoy video chats and instant messaging with webcams and the internet.

This was a massive success: today, there are over 300 million Skype users in the world and a third of all telephone calls are made through Skype. In 2005, Skype was sold to eBay for €2.6 billion, and in 2011, was bought by Microsoft for €8.5 billion. Since then, three other Estonian start ups have become unicorns[17]: Playtech (online games and sports betting), Transferwise (an international money transfer service) and Taxify (now called Bolt) the last one to date. This rival to Uber was created by the Villig brothers, who in 2018 were named the Estonian Entrepreneurs of the Year. On June 29, 2018, Estonian president, Kersti Kaljulaid, proudly Tweeted: "#Estonia is 1.3million people and we have 4 unicorns. There are no other so small countries in the world with 4 unicorns today #NorthernLightThe Skype effect

---

files. In this kind of network, comparable to a client-server network, each client becomes a server. P2P allows for multiple computers to communicate with each other via a network (source JDN).

17. A start up worth over $1 billion+ valuation.

Thanks to this success, Estonians know that they're capable of building companies with a global scope. After its founders sold Skype to eBay, they decided to reinvest in other start ups and feed the nascent ecosystem.

The founding developers of Skype, including Ahti Heinla, launched Ambient Sound, a private investment company. "The effect of Skype was enormous. It's the equivalent of having a couple of world-class universities", says Andrei Korobeinik[18], who created a major social network in Estonia and served as an MP. The company is registered in Luxembourg and has its marketing office in London, but its biggest office and main development team are based in Tallinn. Skype was the first multinational and truly global start up to be created and developed in this relatively small city, which had a colossal impact on the Estonian start up ecosystem. "Companies like Skype are great business for a small country—this changed the entire infrastructure—and had a considerable impact on the ecosystem." The legacy of Skype, combined with the energy and engineering skills of young Estonians, makes Estonia a start up nation, which is in a position to compete with all of Europe.

According to a former Skype employee, "the former Skypers from Estonia and their network had a huge impact: I see a lot of my former colleagues playing leading roles in other start ups and technology companies, Estonian and international, like

18. "The Skype Effect", BBC News, May 13, 2016.

Twillio, Pipedrive, Fleep, MetaMed, Transferwise, Starship..."[19].

As Sten Tamkivi (former head of Skype and founder of Teleport) explains, "we finished by believing that being small gave us an advantage: it wasn't about the size of your staff, but more about finding creative, effective and innovative solutions to a problem. Being small isn't an inconvenience. It just means that you have to think global and to export products from the very beginning. To put it simply, the question, "How can I bring my contribution to the world?" is deeply ingrained in the DNA of your company. Look at the impact that the four former Skype engineers, who were living in Tallinn, have had on the world today."[20]

The former Skypers continue to take on very interesting and different projects. The first employee of Skype, Taavet Hinrikus, took a course at INSEAD (an international business school in Fontainebleau) and then moved to London. In 2011, he and Kristo Käärmann co-founded Transferwise, an online money transfer company, because he was sick of paying high commissions on wire transfers between the UK and Estonia. Transferwise now takes up four floors in a building in Tallinn and handles a billion dollars' worth of international transactions per month. Transferwise investors include Andreessen Horowitz and Peter Thiel's Valar Ventures.

19. *Hacker news*, May 2016.
20. "The Skype Effect", BBC News, May 13, 2016.

Ahti Heinla, another former Skyper, created Starship Technologies with Janus Friis, the Danish co-founder of Skype. The principal investors of the company are Daimler A.G., as well as Shasta Ventures and Matrix Partners from Silicon Valley. Starship builds self-driving robotic delivery vehicles that can carry items within a 6-kilometre radius (otherwise known as "last mile delivery"). Already being tested in multiple cities around the world, the robot is especially suited for pizza delivery.

A start up with global ambitions, Skype has become a teaching base for new skills and a source of inspiration. The Skype effect has also contributed to the creation of a new philosophy, a positive attitude towards future Estonian technology entrepreneurs and a new category of Estonian investors, who have reinvested their profits to create an entire start up ecosystem.

Some former Skype employees have united under the banner "Skype Mafia" (no relation to Skype or Microsoft): they have a website and bring together close to 45 companies whose founders are all former Skypers. Their website declares: "Skype taught us how to build a strong brand, focus on user experience and help make this world a better place. Some of us have now moved on to having an impact through our own independent ventures."

There's also a financial motivation, venture capitalist, Alan Martinson, explains: "If you're in Estonia, and you're technically educated, the only way to become rich in this country is to launch your own company. Unlike in Silicon Valley, it's difficult to get $150,000 salaries in Estonia. Here, you can't get rich living off of a salary, and you can't become rich by just focusing on the Estonian market."[21]

The establishment of numerous start up accelerators and co-working spaces—even real campuses like Tehnopol, which is home to over 200 innovative technology companies—along with the development of a growing community of investors have been crucial to supplying this ecosystem with expertise and capital.

The hashtag #EstonianMafia, which appeared on Twitter in 2012, serves as an example of Estonian start up success. Started by venture capitalist Dave McClure during a competition organised by the seed fund Seedcamp, his Tweet drew attention to the fact that four high-performing Estonian teams were among the competition's 20 finalists.

In order to maintain its status as the birthplace of future successes and to ensure the dynamism of the Estonian start up ecosystem, the government launched its initiative, Startup Estonia. The goal is to make Estonia a start up paradise, by gathering the best people from incubators, accelerators and the private and public sectors into one big family, the digital world's "Estonian Mafia", a term that has become the baseline for the local start up community.

By our count, there are currently around 650 start-ups in Estonia. Most of them operate in the following sectors: business software, services & HR (108 start-ups), AdTech and Creative Tech (98 startups), FinTech (69 startups), HealthTech, Life sciences & Wellness

---

21. "Estonian mafia looking for the next generation of entrepreneurs", Cyrus Farivar, *ArsTechnica*, November 6, 2012.

(58 startups) and CleanTech (48 startups). During the first half of 2019, 35 new startups were established: CyberTech was in the lead, with 10 new startups created this year. The 2019 statistics from the Estonian Tax and Customs Board show that at the end of the second quarter, Estonian startups were employing 4,848 people locally. A year ago, at the end of June 2018, employee numbers had reach 3,369, demonstrating a yearly growth of over 44%! [22].

"The Estonian Wall of Fame"

The co-working space Lift99, which came out of Garage48 (a cornerstone of the start up ecosystem and a hackathon organiser since 2010), is home to the "Estonian Wall of Fame", which features the most prosperous Estonian start ups. To be included in this group of honour, you must have an annual growth of between 80% and 100%, over €3 million in annual revenue or more than €5 million in funding, and pay very high taxes to the Estonian government.

The start ups displayed on the Wall of Fame are:
• Transferwise: peer-to-peer money transfer system;
• Pipedrive: customer relationship management (CRM) software,which was 77th in the Forbes Cloud 100, "tech's hottest category"[23];
• Fortumo: mobile payment solutions;

22. Startup Estonia, 2019.

23. "Estonian-founded Pipedrive in Forbes Cloud 100 list". *Estonian World*, September 16, 2019.

- Taxify: ride-sharing platform in Europe and Africa;
- Lingvist: a language learning software;
- Bondora: a peer-to-peer platform for cross-border lending;
- Testlio: a full-service software and application testing solution;
- Zeroturnaround: developer tools;
- Adcash: online advertising network;
- Skeleton Technology: ultracapacitor-based energy storage;
- Starship: self-driving robotic delivery vehicles;
- Toggl: time tracking system for small businesses;
- Funderbeam: platform for funding and investing through blockchain;
- Monese: mobile app alternative to traditional banking;
- Xolo: online platform for freelancers.

From the start ups that negotiated profitable exits for themselves in 2017, there are:
- Teleport (software for digital nomads, allowing them to live and work wherever is best, according to their personal preferences) which was bought by Move Guides;
- PlanetOS (provider of data infrastructures to help renewable energy companies transform the use of data within their organisations) which was acquired by Intertrust;
- Zeroturnaround (solutions to help Java teams improve their productivity and effectiveness) which was sold to Rogue Wave Software.

In 2017, the biggest employers among start ups were: Transferwise (486 employees), Pipedrive (267), Bolt ex-Taxify (174), Starship Technologies (110) and Cleveron (104).

Governmental initiatives, like the Estonian Startup Visa and the Digital Nomad Visa, reinforce the vitality of this ecosystem:

EU-Startups calls Estonia "the Silicon Valley of Eastern Europe", as the country's tech startup ecosystem continues to grow, with startups raising around €330 million in 2018. The magazine selected 10 exceptionally promising Estonian startups to watch in 2019 and beyond[24]:

• **eAgronom** – Founded in 2016, the Agtech startup provides farmers with a set of convenient and intuitive digital tools to simplify daily and seasonal farm management. Based in Tartu, eAgronom has already expanded to nine countries and is used to manage over 700,000 hectares of grain land, and raised €1 million in 2018.

• **MeetFrank** – This Tallinn-based anonymous HR recruiting app already has 125,000 active users in Estonia, Finland, Sweden, Latvia, Lithuania, and most recently, Germany. Over 2,000 companies currently use MeetFrank's service to attract new employees through its recruiting app. Founded in 2017, MeetFrank raised €1 million in 2018 from Hummingbird VC, Karma VC, and Change Ventures.

• **Modash** – Founded in 2018, this new startup allows marketers to find and collaborate with a

24. "10 Estonian startups to look out for in 2019 and beyond", *EU-Startups*, Janurary 11, 2019.

network of 100 million social media influencers on Twitch and Instagram, in order to build effective influencer marketing campaigns at scale.

- **Nowescape** – Founded in 2016 in Tallinn, Nowescape is like Booking.com – but for escape rooms and other reality games. Nowescape has raised €305k in seed rounds to date.
- **Veriff.me** – Tallinn-based Veriff provides innovative online identity verification solutions to businesses. The startup has developed a way to verify people's identities by analysing videos.
- **Appmediation** – Based in Tallinn with an office in Barcelona and founded in 2017, this smart app monetisation platform was created by experts in data-driven marketing and advertising, and is designed to help app developers fully harness the potential of their inventory.
- **HealthCode AI** – Just founded in 2018 in Tallinn, this startup is developing an AI-based diagnostic platform for physicians. The platform is attempting to address the global shortage of doctors.
- **Withyou** – Based in Tallinn and founded in 2018, this start up relieves the awkwardness of certain social situations and facilitates connection, whether it be in professional networking or dating.
- **Tebo** – This Tallinn-based Edtechstartup allows teachers to organise all of their materials, by uploading their files and creating new ones on its platform.
- **SprayPrinter** – Street artists no longer need to rely on cardboard stencils. SprayPrinter has created a smart spray can technology which projects photos from smartphones onto different surfaces.

We could keep on for a long time as they are numerous astonishing startups, we'll just add two of our personal selection:

• Natufia co-founded by Gregory Lu and Lauri Kapp, is a fully automated bespoke indoor kitchen garden technology allowing to grow pure and tasteful fresh herbs & produce right in everyone's kitchen, anytime of the year, simply and organically and to eat fresh food 24/7.

• ONoff founded by the three-time world champion of ramp roller skating, Taïg Khris. who wants to revolutionize the telecom industry..

The dynamism of the Estonian startup ecosystem was accurately depicted in a hilarious 2019 film called *Chasing Unicorns*[25], which featured fictionalised versions of real people and places. The story is told from the perspective of Õie, a young woman from rural Estonia who stumbles into the Tallinn startup scene before trying to take on the world with her own tech company. The movie was shot in the summer of 2018 in Estonia and California, and many of the scenes took place in Telliskivi, Tallinn's creative hub. The director, Rain Rannu, is an Estonian entrepreneur-turned-filmmaker (he founded a successful mobile payment company, Fortumo) and the movie is based on the real experiences of over 30 Estonian entrepreneurs. There are plans to distribute the movie internationally.

---

25. "Chasing Unicorns: A hilarious new movie about Estonian entrepreneurs taking on the world", Adam Rang. *Estonian World*, September 14, 2019.

Estonian Startup Via

The Estonian Startup Visa, which was launched 2years ago by the local startup community, Estonia's Ministry of the Interior and Startup Estonia, enables non-European expats to work for Estonian start ups, relocate their existing start ups or create new ones in Estonia.

This visa can be issued for a total of 18 months. For a longer stay, a temporary visa can be requested, and a temporary residence permit for entrepreneurship can be issued for up to five years.

"The Estonian Startup Visa team has noticed that the people who benefit from this programme often wish to extend their stay. Many have requested residence permits to be able to stay on after 18 months," explains Merilin Lukk, project manager at Estonian Startup Visa.[26] Entrepreneurs can come with their families. "If you obtain a Startup Visa, your partner and children can also come with you. With this visa, your partner will even have the right to work, for a limited period of time."[27]

Digital Nomad Visa

Killu Vantsi, adviser at the Citizenship and Migration Policy Department of the Ministry of the Interior, announced that the new Digital Nomad Visa launched

---

26. startupvisa.ee.
27. *Life in Estonia*, February 2018.

at the beginning of 2019 and would bring 1,400 people to Estonia every year. This new visa would grant young entrepreneurs and workers from outside the EU who are temporarily living in Estonia the right to reside in the country for 365 days and to obtain a Schengen Visa, which would allow them to visit member countries for a maximum stay of 90 days. This flexible visa policy helps attract the best talents and significantly raises the stakes of international competition. Many Silicon Valley entrepreneurs have stated that overly restrictive visa policies from the federal government—even before the election of Donald Trump—have deprived them of numerous talented people.

Training, the cornerstone of the ecosystem

The start up ecosystem is supported by top-quality training anda great deal of fluidity within the working world. At a time when parts of Europe are struggling to acquire the technical skills needed to technologically advance, Estonia is widely recognised for the quality (and quantity) of the coders it trains.

Schools and universities teach engineering, robotics and programming with a mindset that's halfway between creative and scientific. This foundational training policy pays off: one out of ten students in Estonia will pursue a career in new information and communications technology, double the OECD average. Education is just as important. First employee of Skype and cofounder of Transferwise, Taavet Hinrikus, states, "In the 1980s, every single high school student wanted to be a rock star. Now in high schools, everyone wants to be an entrepreneur."[28]

For Charles-Henri Hirsch, one of the founders of Eurostep Digital (an online exchange market for companies that are unlisted on the stock exchange), "Estonia has quickly appeared as a good compromise between a breeding ground for specialised skills and a very attractive administrative and financial environment. Financially, since the tax rate is 20% on profits and 0% if the profits are reinvested in the company, and administratively because of how easy it is to create and manage a company."

"In a country where kids learn to code by the first grade, it was only a matter of time before startups began to sprout", writes Conor Grant, who describes Estonia as "Eastern Europe's self-made unicorn pasture".[29]

Estonian president, Kersti Kaljulaid, sums up the situation well: "Our small country has only one natural resource and it's located between our ears. That is completely clear. Therefore, education that is accessible to all children, regardless of their parents' living or work choices, is a good thing—we have it today and we must keep it."[30]

---

28. "How did Estonia become a leader in technology? By ditching legacy technology and betting on education", *The Economist*, July 31, 2013.

29. "Tech-savvy Estonia wants you to know it has 1.3m people — and 4 unicorns", *The Hustle*, July 5, 2018.

30. "A small country has only one natural resource - between our ears", Kersti Kaljulaid, *Estonian world*, February 24, 2017, published in 2018.

E-Residency, the new digital nation for the entrepreneurs of the world

"Our country is located very high up, at the eastern border of the European Union. This doesn't work out great with our Russian neighbour and the local population is slowly diminishing... This means that we must absolutely find ideas to keep the economy going and find new clients. So, why not attract them to us with the digital?" asks Taavi Kotka[31], former Chief Information Officer of the Estonian Government, who worked extensively on the creation of the e-Residency programme. The e-Residency programme (or digital transnationality) was born out of a government-sponsored hackathon in 2014. Today, the State start up is in beta testing and has a stated objective of 10 million e-Residents by 2025.

From anywhere in the world, e-Residents can access Estonian digital services, create businesses in Estonia, fully manage them online, electronically sign documents, and gain access to professional banking services and international online payment systems, all without ever needing to go to Estonia. E-Residency requests are made online and cost€100. You then retrieve your card from the Estonian Embassy, where your fingerprints will be taken to complete the identification process. Specialised service providers handle your fiscal residence and accounts.

---

31. "L'Estonie, le pays des 'e-citoyens'" [Estonia, the country of 'e-citizens'], *Les Echos*, February 10, 2016.

In January 2018, the designation of an on-site legal company representative was made mandatory. Once this is done, the company can be fully managed remotely. To do so, there are two options: if the e-Resident wants to open an account in a traditional Estonian bank, they must go to the physical location, explain their business plan and provide proof of economic ties with Estonia. Their being able to open an account depends entirely on the bank's internal policies and decision. The second option is for the e-Resident to use the banking services of a Fintech company (Holvi, which has a partnership with the programme, Payoneer, Transferwise Borderless account, etc.). This is why access to professional banking services is guaranteed, but not the opening of a bank account.

At the 2014 launch, the British journalist Edward Lucas, a frequent traveller in the Baltic countries, received the very first e-Resident card from the hands of former President Toomas Hendrik Ilves. Others followed, including Americans Tim Draper, a venture capital magnate, and Guy Kawasaki, one of the marketing pioneers at Apple. Shinzo Abe(the Prime Minister of Japan), Angela Merkel and Xavier Bettel (Prime Minister of Luxembourg)[32], Bill Gates (Microsoft founder and former CEO) and Pope Francis also received their cards.

E-Residency boasts a very ambitious political programme, which rests on the conviction that digital technology increases borderless entrepreneurship

32. "L'Estonie, le pays des 'e-citoyens'", *Les Echos*, February 10, 2016.

opportunities. E-Residency claims to be the following:

• Inclusive: anyone on the planet can become an e-Resident (subject to police checks at borders and customs).

• Legitimate: e-Residency gives entrepreneurs access to a European business environment. Each company has the same rights as any Estonian company.

• Transparent: access to personal data is monitored. Each e-Resident knows which administration is looking at their data. There is constant information exchange with the administrations of all involved countries, especially when it comes to finances.

• Emancipating: e-Residency democratises access to entrepreneurship across the globe.

This official message is coupled with a universal vision that reinforces what Estonia can bring to the world, thanks to digital technology.

Kaspar Korjus, former Managing Director of the e-Residency programme[33], whom we met in May 2017 during the Latitude59 conference, told us: "Two and a half years ago, we decided to become a nation without borders so that any citizen on the planet could become an e-Resident of Estonia and create their company, all while staying near their loved ones and in their country. Our goal is to help improve the world with the creation of new products and services. The problem isn't a lack of ideas

---

33. Now co-founder of Pactum, an AI-based system that helps global companies autonomously offer personalised, commercial negotiations on a massive scale.

or talent: the main problem comes from red tape and financial constraints. What entrepreneurs need is the ability to create and manage an enterprise that generates trust in the whole world with online management tools like integrated banking services and international payment solutions."[34] A study published by Deloitte in December 2017[35]reports that during the first three years of the programme's existence, e-Residents brought €14.4 million into Estonia and that this number would reach 1.8 billion by 2025, meaning a return of €100 for each Euro invested in the programme. Before then, the team hopes to have 150,000 e-Residents and 20,000 companies by 2020. "E-Residency is most beneficial to business people outside the EU who want access to the EU single market, and to freelancers, especially from emerging markets, who need to accept online credit card payments, but who currently don't have access to this in their countries," says Arnaud Castaignet. Former Digital Strategist and Communications Officer for François Hollande, Castaignet was Head of Public Relations for the e-Residency programme from 2017 to 2019. "This programme benefits digital nomads who want to travel the world and fully manage their companies online from wherever they happen to be; entrepreneurs who want to have access to a lot of capital; and business people inside the EU who want to lower their

---

34. Interview with the authors, used in "L'entrepreneur sans frontière" [The entrepreneur without borders] on the blog *Le Meunier Qui Dort*, May 2017.

35. *E-Residency brought €14.4 million to Estonia in first three years*, Deloitte, December 2017.

companies' administration costs."[36]He goes on to explain: "In particular, we target entrepreneurs and freelancers, but NGOs, volunteer associations, non-profits, research institutions, etcetera, can all profit from e-Residency. They also could find it easier to manage their activities via an administration that's agile and simple."[37]

From innovative solutions to entrepreneurs without borders

Who are e-Residents?
The programme's aim is to attract capital into the country. It targets digital nomads, freelancers and all entrepreneurs looking to manage their business activities remotely, within an environment supported by a minimalist administration.

The following are just some of the e-Residents who have created their own companies:

Arzu is a professional tour guide from Istanbul who created Walks in Istanbul. In 2015, she sold over 600 walking tours and employed 12 local guides. However, political problems in the region led to a sharp drop in tourism. PayPal soon stopped operating in Turkey, so even if tourists wanted to use her services, they couldn't pay. Arzu found out about

---

36. "Why Estonia succeeds at public innovation", *US News* (Best countriesrankings), February 8, 2018.

37. "Devenir e-Resident : comment la nationalité numérique fait rayonnerl 'Estonie" [Becoming an e-Resident: how digital nationality makes Estonia shine], *Mashable*, October 4, 2017.

e-Residency and created Walks in Europe. With her new European company, she had access to international payment providers and could also develop her business activities on the continent.[38]

Oleg Savanovich, originally from Russia, created Telexchange System, one of the highest performing telecommunications companies registered in Estonia. He's been managing his company online from Sweden where he lives. E-Residency has helped him reduce his operating costs and provide greater added value for his clients.

Deepak Solanki lives in India. He developed LiFi—an innovative alternative to WiFi—through the intermediary of his company Velmenni. He started the company in India but he had difficulty raising funds until he'd established it in the European Union, thanks to Estonia. The company is now managed remotely, thanks to e-Residency, and has found investors in the United Kingdom and Zimbabwe, who have all also become e-Residents.[39]

Vicky Brock, an entrepreneur from northern England, created the start up Vistalworks, which helpsprotect consumers from criminals attempting to rob them or sell them fake and dangerous goods online. Her company offers a free service for checking products on eBay and is also preparing to launch a free browser plug-in that will protect consumers as they shop on

---

38. e-resident.gov.ee.

39. "Who are Estonia's e-Residents? Estonia became the first country to offer e-Residency 3 years ago & now has nearly 30,000 people from 139 countries signed up", Adam Rang, *Medium*, November 30, 2017.

the web: this plug- in will automatically alert them to any potential threat by using data algorithms and a blacklist of any website that is known to have already ripped off consumers. Vicky teamed up with her husband, Stephen Budd and another entrepreneur named Alan Murray to launch Vistalworks, which is mainly based in Scotland.

The startup won the Civic Innovation Challenge, and its three primary revenue sources are the types of organisations that are on the frontline of battling illicit trade: public bodies (like Vistalworks' first customers), online marketplaces and financial services. These three groups all require more data in order to tackle the problem, which Vistalworks can provide without giving away any personal user data. "We don't collect any personal information about consumers, but we understand broader shopping patterns and can see where the criminals are lurking."Vistalworks was initially established in Scotland as a UK company and now has 10 employees working in Glasgow and Edinburgh.

Vicky and Stephen are both e-Residents of Estonia, and have used the programme to make Vistalworksan EU company too, which will operate in parallel with its UK version. It will focus on international business development and localise the tools for additional markets beyond the UK. This wouldn't have happened, Vicky says, were it not for Brexit.[40]

---

40. "British entrepreneur Vicky Brock is using e-Residency to protect consumers from online crime", Adam Rang,

More and more e-Residents

The number of e-Residents is growing quickly; by 2017, there were more new e-Residents than there were births. "Ernest Hemingway once wrote: 'In every port in the world, at least two Estonians can be found.' However, it's now even easier to find everywhere you go e-Residents from our digital nation," explains Silver Siniavski, Project Manager of e-Residency.[41]

By its five-year anniversary in December 2019, e-Residency has grown to become a community of nearly 60,000 digitally empowered citizens from 162 countries. The initiative has led to the creation of over 10,000 businesses and the investment of millions of euros into the Estonian economy, thus demonstrating how being digitally advanced has opened doors for Estonia to become more self-sufficient and make a name for itself amongst some of the other European powerhouses.

The most represented countries among e-Residents are Finland, Russia and Ukraine. The announcement of Brexit boosted the number of requests from the UK. As Adam Rang noted in the blog *Medium* on January 26, 2018, around 30,000 British companies have websites with the domain name ".eu", which they will lose the right to use in 2019, unless they become Estonian e-Residents.

For Geoffroy Berson, former Attaché for Coope-ration on Digital Innovation at the French Institute

---

41. "There's an app for that (launching summer 2018). Our new community network will give e-Residents more opportunities to connect, learn and grow companies, E-Residency", *Medium*.

of Estonia in Tallinn, "e-Residency is also a show-case to the international world of the State's agile methods".[42] "E-Residency is doing for countries what start ups are doing for corporations," confirms Karoli Hindriks, CEO of Jobbatical. "By lowering the barriers to establish a company in the country and making it easier for international entrepreneurs to access its infrastructure, it could be argued that the e-Residency scheme is disrupting the idea of nationality itself. The openness to taking a risk like that is a very good reflection of the mindset that you see in Estonia."[43]

A multi-faceted programme

eTrade for all
The e-Residency programme is connected with the United Nations Conference on Trade and Development (UNCTAD) and other international organisations around the initiative "e-Trade for all", which wants to help clear the way for global growth by allowing more people to create companies online.

One of the first examples of this idea of e-commerce for everyone involves women in Delhi, India. The Indian Institute of Technology in Delhi launched an initiative called Women Entrepreneurship and Empowerment (WEE), which is supported by the Indian government's Department of Science & Technology. Participants receive local business

---

42. Interview with the authors.

43. "How Tallinn's tech talent transformed its startup ecosystem on Thursday", *elitebusiness*, January 18, 2018.

mentoring, as well as an e-Residency in Estonia, in order to start their company.

A programme in constant evolution

"Today, the direct economic impact of e-Residency is 14 million Euros. It is profitable as a programme, but the indirect value that the programme creates (people discovering Estonia as a travel destination, investing in the country, etc.) is much more significant for Estonia. Through e-Residency we share our expertise in creating digital solutions and making life easier for everybody. The growing network of e-residents' companies and service providers are creating jobs for a variety of specialists both in Estonia and abroad. E-Residency is a platform to empower starting entrepreneurs and give them access to a hassle-free taxation system and a supportive environment. E-Residency represents the values of our economy such as transparency and resourcefulness, and the values of our nation such as openness, sustainability and cooperation." says, Ott Vatter[44], Managing Director of e-Residency.

The e-Residency teams are never outdone when it comes to innovation: a new initiative called e-Residency 2.0 was launched with Estonian president, Kersti Kaljulaid. The initiative's white paper contains 49 recommendations and aims to ensure that e-Residency will become even more beneficial for Estonian citizens, no matter where they live,

---

44. "Estonia's E-Residency Contributed €14M To Its Economy--'E-Residency 2.0 Will Be A True Forerunner'", *Forbes*, April 25, 2019.

Estonian residents and, of course, the e-Residents themselves.

"E-Residency 2.0 will go further and aims to be a true forerunner in terms of digital transformation. We will focus on the quality rather than quantity, working to make e-Residents' business lives as hassle-free as possible whilst also providing them better networking options and giving them more tools to grow their average company value. For Estonia, it means exporting our knowledge, culture and way of life to like-minded people across the globe", adds Vatter[45].

For now, the programme will focus on businesses and technology, but in the future, culture will also play a role.

On or offshore?

From the outside, the Estonian e-Residency system could be seen as an attempt to attract business development through financial incentives. However, this isn't an invitation to tax avoidance: even in this country of enterprise and profits, companies must still pay taxes.

This is what Dmitri Jegorov, the Deputy Secretary-General for Tax and Customs Policies at the Estonian Ministry of Finance, emphasises[46]:

"Certain people started to think that the e-Residency programme could help them avoid tax

45. "Estonia's E-Residency Contributed €14M To Its Economy--'E-Residency 2.0 Will Be A True Forerunner'", *Forbes*, April 25, 2019.

46. Interview with the authors.

responsibilities, but the Estonian government stood firm: while the e-Residency programme encourages people to start their own companies and helps them get access to the European market, Estonia is not a tax haven. E-Residency can always be revoked.

E-Residents are subject to the same tax system as Estonians. This means that there's a 20% tax for all companies, although only distributed profits, and not revenue, are subject to taxation, which makes it fundamentally different from the rest of the world. However, if a company does most of its business in a foreign country, the tax laws of that country apply. For example, if the e-Resident owner of an Estonian company comes from country A and sells services to businesses or individuals in country A, all while being directly and actively involved in almost 100% of the commercial activities of the company, that owner will most likely have to enter into a more established set-up in country A, and will have to pay income tax, based on the earned profits.

However, there are many companies in Estonia, which are held and managed by foreign e-Residents, and are sometimes very active locally. The main reason for this is the ease that the administrative framework allows, when it comes to signing contracts, submitting reports to the States and completing all other steps remotely. These are legal Estonian companies, without any particular risks when it comes to international taxation.

In Estonia, our national laws also help us avoid double taxation. This means that if taxes must be paid in a foreign country, according to a foreign law or bilateral treaty, this tax is, in most cases, deductible in Estonia and there is no double tax. We've never had the intention of being an offshore financial centre: only legal companies are welcome here."

The decisions of the Court of Justice of the European Union have upheld this compliance with the European legal system, on multiple occasions.

A programme that inspires

E-Residency inspired Azerbaijan to create an equivalent programme. Lithuania and Kazakhstan have made announcements that they'll be following its example. Ott Vatter[47]wrote: "A universal desire for a more connected world can bring countries together by promoting borderless working through programmes such as e-Residency, serving a unified rather than divided global mission. It's only a matter of time until the UK offers its own version of e-Residency in order to export its business environment and culture – and ultimately make more friends around the world"[48].

Kaspar Korjus[49]encourages the competition: "We're happy to see this kind of initiative, because it's in keeping with our philosophy. We want to help promote high-quality services for everyone, and so the more actors there are, the more people can benefit!"[50]

This new Estonian universalism is always on display!

---

47. Managing Director of e-Residency.

48. "Why Estonia pioneered digital identity",*TechRadar*, September3, 2019.

49. Former director of the e-Residency programme,

50. « L'entrepreneur sans frontière » [The entrepreneur without borders], *Le Meunier Qui Dort*, May 2017.

6. E-Estonia:
Marketing Strategy
or Exportable Model?

Estonia and Estonians have legitimate reasons for being proud, given how highly Estonia is placed in different international rankings, both public and private.

E-Estonia is a frontrunner in multiple areas:

- Number 1 in Europe for digital economy, society and public services (European Commission's Digital Economy and Society Index(2017)
- Number 1 in the world for entrepreneurship (World Economic Forum)
- Number 1 in global digital development(Barclays Digital Development Index)
- Number 1 in the world for mobile network coverage (Global Information Technology Report)
- Number 1 in Europe in cybersecurity (International Telecommunication Union)
- Number 1 in the world in tax competitiveness (OECD)
- Number 1 in the world for tax collection in 2017 (International Tax Competitiveness Index of the Tax Foundation)

- Number 1 in Europe and Number 3 globally (PISA education rankings)
- Number 1 for digital life (InterNations 2019): "The country is rated best in the world for both unrestricted access to online services (e.g. social media) and the availability of administrative or government services online."[1]
- Most recently, Estonia won the Master of Reinvention Award at the 2019 London Business School of Economics (LSE) Real Innovation Awards. It was especially recognised for its successful implementation of e-Identity and the e-Residency programme, as well as its status as a start up country.[2]

According to a report from Freedom House, Estonia remains the most connected country in the world and Estonian users encounter very few obstacles to internet access.

In its annual rankings, the independent German foundation Bertelsmann Stiftung places Estonia second in terms of economic transformation. According to the index, Estonia has largely recovered from the 2008-2009 economic recession, thanks to its capacity for innovation and the effectiveness of its public and private sectors.

In 2018, the Estonian government received a leadership prize at the GSMA Mobile World Congress's global convention in Barcelona.[3] The jury praised the

---

1. "Estonia declared the best country for digital life", *Estonian World*, May 30, 2019.

2. e-estonia.com, November 2019.

3. The GSMA represents the interests of mobile telephone operators across the globe. It gathers together close to 800 operators and over

political approaches adopted by the Estonian government to support the deployment of mobile services, especially when it came to supplying fibre optics in rural areas and actively promoting and quickly developing 5G services.

This kind of appreciation is crucial for a country that's only 26 years old. As Paul Regnard[4], who completed the international trainee programme VIE (*Volontariat International en Entreprises*) in Tallinn recalls, "we were always surprised by how little time had passed since the return of independence in 1991, which we remembered every time we saw the cross of the obelisk [part of the Maarjamäe Memorial]". This success is lived like a shared realisation, or even better, the proof of something that sets Estonia apart from its neighbours, thereby guaranteeing that it will never be forgotten as a nation.

"After the German and Soviet occupations, we finally have our own administration, the result of our intellect. We're very proud of that. And it's all that we have," explains Anto Veldre, who works at RIA, the agency that pilots the State's IT systems.

For Estonia, this digital model is at once inseparable from how its liberal democracy was built and a strong marker of identity for a country that wants, at all costs, to free itself from any association with the Baltic countries and even Eastern Europe. The State's digital model, where the citizen is central,

---

300 companies within the mobile ecosystem, including telephone and device manufacturers, software companies, equipment suppliers and internet companies, as well as organisations from adjacent industrial sectors. Source: www.mobileworldcongress.com

4.   Interview with the authors.

and the start-up oriented digital State itself are both significant as factors that differentiate Estonia from its neighbours to the East.

All of this plays a decisive role in solidifying the feeling of national reassurance. The genius of Estonia has always been its language. Among recent Estonian literary successes are *The Man Who Spoke Snakish* by Andrus Kivirähk (so well known that it inspired the creation of a popular board game); *Purge*, written by Sofi Oksanen and recipient of the 2010 French Prix Fémina; and *Un roman estonien* (An Estonian Novel) by Katrina Kalda.

The globally renowned composer Arvo Pärt is at the head of the list of famous Estonians, although more recently, rapper Tommy Cash has been developing a notoriety that extends beyond the country's borders.

Modern Estonian genius is exemplified by its digital success stories and the digital State itself, as the Estonian president confirms: "The digital State is what makes Estonia exceptional". Barack Obama understood this. When he visited Tallinn in September 2014, he remarked, "I should have called the Estonians when we were setting up our health care website!" Wonderful recognition for Estonia's digital uniqueness!

While this digital framework is a source of national pride, it also helps ground the country within systems like that of the European Union: Estonia's presidency of the EU allowed it to use the Tallinn Digital Summit in September 2017 as a platform for its digital model. As Russia increasingly proves to be a threat, it also functions as one more security measure, after NATO and the EU, another way of reminding everyone of Estonia's existence.

It's notable that Estonia and the UK, along with Israel, South Korea and New Zealand, are the founding members of Digital 5, which became Digital 7 after Canada and Uruguay joined, and then Digital 9 with the additions of Portugal and Mexico. D9 is a network of high-profile digital governments, which aims to reinforce the digital economy. The members are tied to each other by the principle of openness. They focus their efforts on the changing relationship between government and technology, by adopting open standards and free software, and working to make digital governments faster and more effective.

Performing the Estonian model

E-Estonia is a brand with a perfect marketing strategy. Everything about it is very precise, including the discourse units, visuals and typography. The unity of vision amongst the promoters of this model is impressive and could become a case study for future communications students. The Estonian model certainly exists but it's also constantly being performed for others, thanks to the efforts of a governmental agency dedicated to e-Estonia and its showroom (whose humorous marketing strategy presents the country as being "the coolest digital society").

These are the kinds of formulas that one can find in official presentations: "Estonia is one of the most advanced e-Societies in the world. Its exceptional success was made possible through the efforts of its pioneering government, its proactive ICT sector and its population's strong interest in technology." It's true that visionary political choices have encouraged the population's excitement about digital technology: not an easy thing to do, as we've already discussed...

An exportable model

The e-Governance Academy is both a think tank and an advisory body, which celebrated 15 years of existence in 2017. The organisation teaches good practices in e-Governance, e-Democracy, open information societies and national cybersecurity. Its activities are concentrated around three poles: training, guidance and research. The e-Governance Academy has already trained over 3,500 civil servants from more than 60 countries around the world.

Ukraine, Finland, Norway, Georgia, Denmark, Palestine, Azerbaijan and 18 African countries are working on adapting their own versions of X-Road. Greece is interested in how electronic signatures can help fight fraud, Nigeria has worked with Estonia on the taxation portal, and Qatar is cooperating with Estonia on a general public services portal. Large countries like Canada are seriously considering the use of X-Road and India is examining its health portal.

If X-Road isn't being duplicated in these countries, it's being developed as an intermediary between existing systems and users.

The e-Governance Academy is also planning to launch an online development platform in 2019 that will be used to train over 10,000 civil servants in Ukraine's local government. This training will take place within the context of administrative reform, which will give new functions to local administrations, related to their incomes, social services and important transactions involving data, which up until now were handled by the central government. The platform was created in partnership with BCS Koolitus, the Estonian IT sector's main training and project management company. It was developed within the framework of the U-LEAD programme, with assistance from GIZ, a German development cooperation organisation that supports education and sustainable development activities throughout the world.

This exporting of its model should also make Estonia question itself, according to the political science researcher Kadi Maria Vooglaid[5]: "This is the second lesson to learn from e-Estonia—the use of technology is never value-neutral, and it is especially important in the context of governance. The fact that the Estonian e-Government was built parallel to building a newly liberal democratic nation, means that the whole process resulted in an infrastructure, both legal and technological, which places not only the needs of the people, but also the rights and privacy of its citizens above all. The Estonian experience in exporting our e-Government technologies, along with the examples of countries like China and Singapore, demonstrate that e-Government can also be used to curb rights and abolish privacy.

---

5. "What should be the state's role in a digital future?", *Estonian world*, January 2018.

There's also a lesson for Estonia here: if the discourse surrounding e-Government in Estonia routinely fails to take into account political and social values embedded in the use and development of technologies in government, we might one day discover that we've taken the wrong turn, and it'll be difficult to backtrack once systems are in place. Therefore, the State still matters, because it's the central concept governing our debates about how we organise life in a society. And these debates will always matter, no matter how much the State has managed to eliminate itself via technology."

Countries are not the only ones facing the challenges of digital transformation: Estonia is also exporting its expertise to international organisations which are undergoing reform processes and looking into innovative ways to deliver their mandate and services. Several international organisations, including the IOM (International Organisation for Migration), the UNHCR (United Nations High Commissioner for Refugees), the OHCHR (Office of the United Nations High Commissioner for Human Rights)and the ICRC (International Committee of the Red Cross), participated in the Tallinn Digital Summit on September 17, 2019, in the hopes of gaining more information about the Estonian experience. In fact, as the entire UN System continues to confront this challenge, Estonian experience will be particularly useful when it comes to cybersecurity, interoperability, biometrics and digital IDs.

Estonia has also signed a Memorandum of Understanding with the United Nations Development

Programme (UNDP) in order to use digital transformation as a means of achieving the Sustainable Development Goals (SDG). The expected outcome of the project, which was launched in 2018, is to accelerate structural transformations for sustainable development. The project aims to increase support to developing countries, by transforming their digital landscapes so as to bring them closer to SDG fulfilment, and to strengthen the UNDP's ability to more effectively provide this support.

The program leverages the UNDP's global platform (as well as its presence in about 170 countries and territories) to share Estonia's e-Governance experience and the expertise of the Estonian e-Governance Academy (the implementing body on the Estonian side): their combined potential will help enable the acceleration of development. The cooperation involves four distinct work streams:

1. Develop a practical tool for rapid assessment of digital landscapes and support its application;

2. Transform the UNDP's digital capabilities to better support countries;

3. Build in-country digital literacy knowledge bases, capacities and competencies;

4. e-Identity and Smart Cities.

This last example shows that what Estonia is exporting is an expertise, rather than a ready-to-duplicate template. Can Estonian model be duplicated at any scale?

Faced with the success of the Estonian model, a lot of countries are divided into multiple categories: those who wish to reproduce it, those who wish to be inspired by it...and those who acknowledge this success, while also pointing out that this kind of e-Government could only be built in a small country with a short history. And yet, when one asks Estonians if it's possible to implement X-Road in a big country, they roll their eyes and answer, "Of course it is! Developing it on a larger scale isn't a problem nowadays!"

For Kadi Maria Vooglaid, we also mustn't forget that "the techno-legal paradigm in place in the government today depends upon a robust interplay of several unique aspects of the historical, socio-political and cultural context of Estonia, such as the lack of legacy systems in the bureaucracy or stable cross-partisanship". This isn't to say that the model can't be duplicated elsewhere, but that we must have a deeper understanding of its foundations, which do not rely solely on technology.

As Linnar Viik, one of the founders of the e-Governance Academy, reminds us[6]: "E-Governance isn't so much a question of technology, as there are other crucial aspects: laws, conviction, the confidence and knowledge to be able to convince in order to generate support." When discussing countries with old administrations, which cannot start from scratch, former Estonian president Ilves maintains, "Estonia's success doesn't depend so much on abandoning inherited technology as it does on abandoning 'traditional thinking'."[7]

---

6.   *Life in Estonia*, February 2018.

7.   e-estonia.

The concept of "Government as a Platform"

In 2009, Irish-American author, editor and IT specialist Tim O'Reilly, who coined the term "Web 2.0", wrote the seminal article entitled "Government as a Platform"[8] in which he took the platform development lessons learned in the digital era to suggest ways in which to improve the effectiveness of the State. Here, he sets up the foundation and structure for the concept of the State as a platform.

This theory was the subject of a study entitled "Government as a platform: what can Estonia show the world?", which was led in 2016 by Helen Margetts and Andre Naumann for the Oxford Internet Institute of Oxford University.[9] The two academics analysed the principles behind the idea of government as a platform through the prism of a comparative study between British and Estonian approaches.

The following are some of the most illuminating excerpts.

"The notion of government as a platform (GaaP) offers to encapsulate the use of digital technologies to support the resolution of collective action problems at various levels (city, county, national, regional) through shared software, data and services—and thereby improve the efficiency and effectiveness of government and governance, doing more for less.

The principle foundations of this notion are: openness, simplicity, participation, 'learning from

---

8. *MIT Press Journal*, July 18, 2011.

9. 2017 Oxford University research paper.

hackers', data mining, experimentation and 'leading by example'. In this model, Tim O'Reilly considers government as a 'convener and enabler' rather than the first mover of civic action. According to him, government should develop the capacity to innovate in an 'ecosystem of participation' by asking two key questions:

1. How does government become an open platform that allows people inside and outside government to innovate?

2. How do you design a system in which the outcomes are not determined beforehand, but evolve through interactions between government and its citizens?

Starting in 2010, the conservative government of the United Kingdom decided to give significant means to the State's digital programmes, with a new central organisation, the Government Digital Service (GDS) directed by Mike Bracken, and a strong objective: Digital by Default. This dynamic was also driven by the goal of reducing public spending and the desire to 'do more for less'.

Between 2010 and 2015, the creation of the GDS allowed for £1.7 billion in savings. The successes were also organisational, with GDS being the sole actor to work across all the different departments, facilitating projects, involved in every hiring decision for senior digital staff, raising the quality and capacity of digital expertise. GDS could also review contracts, services and the IT organisations of all public ministries and organisations. All of these actions led to the insourcing of some functions at lower costs, the building up of capacity across the civil service, the embrace of the open-source movement and putting back on the right track certain underperforming government IT projects. GDS championed the Government as a Platform approach and, in the 2015 spending review, GDS received a major vote of confidence in the form of £450 million, with GaaP mentioned explicitly.

UK-style GaaP has been very different from Estonia, however. There is no equivalent of X-Road: the largest departments operate their own databases with few links between them. There is no centralised e-ID system or ID card. The National Insurance number, the closest thing that the UK has to a unique personal identifier, is issued only when a citizen starts to work, rather than at birth, as in Estonia. The building blocks of the UK GaaP approach are Verify, a federated identity system that does not require ID, Govpay for making payments to the government and Notify for government agencies to notify citizens of progress on services. The most obvious GaaP feature is an official government portal for interacting with services, www.gov.uk.

This policy was one of radical centralisation, to have all the content controlled from the centre and only the back-end services going through to departments, and it has caught international attention. Mike Bracken wooed the world with his talk of 'beautiful public services', bringing concepts like quality, innovation and robustness back into government, akin to the progressive public administration of the post-war era.

These successes have engendered, not only a procession of overseas visitors coming to seek out inspiration, but also imitations across the world, from Australia to the United States, where the recently created United States Digital Service in the Executive Office of the President is a direct reproduction of GDS. In 2013, the UK also signed a memorandum of understanding with Estonia, representing 'a commitment by the two countries to work together on developing public services that are digital by default'.

In 2016, the UK saw its efforts rewarded, with the country leading the UN rankings for digital government, just as Estonia was slipping down to a middling position. Even Estonia is looking to replicate some elements of www.gov.uk in the development of their central portal. But in Great Britain, there is little chance of the development of the other 'layers' of GaaP that have brought Estonia success.

The weaknesses of the British GaaP approach are visible. Although the Estonian model has been much admired in the UK and a system of data registries discussed as the best way to go since the earliest days of GDS, these have not got much past the discussion stage. Additionally, there are few signs that open data is being used by either citizens or enterprises to make government more transparent or to improve government services. So, the UK version of the openness principle is partial at best, and cannot really be seen as characterising UK digital government, as it does in Estonia. One of the other weaknesses of the model from across the Channel is the absence of shared services across the bigger departments, as each is still developing its own programmes, despite the coordination efforts of GDS.

Ironically, the country that has explicitly aimed to implement the GaaP model seems to be far further from achieving it than Estonia, where some kind of platform vision seems to have materialised, although not explicitly articulated along the way. Nevertheless, Estonia is closer than any other to achieving the GaaP vision, since the three 'layers' of a platform have been defined since 1999: a shared data system (X-Road), unique access (e-ID) and access to a layer of services via multiple portals (eesti.ee). It's these three levels that handle, simultaneously, the public and private sectors and are responsible for Estonia's reputation as a digital State, but which also make it an example, by breaking down preconceptions about the inability of States to innovate."

What about France?

Estonia's holding of the presidency of the Council of the European Union in the second half of 2017 led to numerous French ministerial visits to Estonia where the virtues of the local model of e-Government were extolled.

However, France is far from having its own model of Government as a Platform: there is no single, distributed infrastructure (like X-Road), no unique identification system (like e-ID), and not even a portal to access services. The building blocks for such a model do exist, including online tax declaration and medical file access, but there is no general programme.

Justifying arguments often point to the complexity of France's administration, which is much bigger than that of Estonia (2% of the Estonian population is civil servants, compared to 9% of the population in France); the historical legacy, which is much harder to ignore than that of a more recent State; the difference in demographic weight; and the reluctance of the French population to use online services. Being able to start from a completely clean slate when making the move towards the digital makes it much easier to adopt digital technologies in an agile and innovative manner, rather than having to completely overhaul an existing system in order to facilitate total digital transformation, which is what would be required in France. And yet, the failure of certain projects in France, like the electronic ID card, which has been considered on multiple occasions, has nothing to do with the size of the country, nor how long its administrative culture has existed!

In order to understand the true issues and motivations behind the digital transformation of a State, we spoke to Estonians and to French people who have lived in Estonia about what it would take for France to achieve the Estonian model.

For Kaspar Korjus, former Managing Director of the e-Residency programme, "You should ask your country to go digital! The request has to come from French citizens; they must demand that the State completely digitises itself. They shouldn't be afraid. This digital system is a lot more secure than an administration founded on paper. You begin by establishing trust, raising social awareness and passing laws. The technology part happens afterwards."[10] Close to 40% of the French population still feels anxiety when faced with the prospect of the administration's digital transformation[11], which shows that there's still a lot more educating work that needs to be done.

For Geoffroy Berson (former Attaché for Cooperation on Digital Innovation at the French Institute of Estonia in Tallinn), "the comparison with the French situation is striking, where the problem of dead zones [areas not covered by a mobile network] reminds us that having an internet connection has always been an important factor when thinking about inequalities in a given territory, and those are the places where talk of digitising services really worries the population. Here, we think that e-Services make each citizen equal in the eyes of the State; but that's only been possible because of a significant rollout of high-speed networks."[12]The State as a platform is only possible once the proper infrastructural conditions have been put in place.

For Pierre Gronlier, who was an engineer at Skype, the French problem is also linked to total ignorance of digital tools: "When you look at all of the current security measures, how could anyone think that an e-mail sent through an SSL connection is less secure than a signed paper letter that a 14-year-old could

10. « L'entrepreneur sans frontière » [The entrepreneur withoutborders], Le Meunier Qui Dort, May 2017.

11. « L'e-administration, un objectif plus facile à dire qu'à atteindre » [E-Administration, easiersaidthandone], *earchimag.com*, February 7, 2018.

12. Interview with the authors.

forge using Photoshop?"[13] Education and training play equally central roles in the adoption of digital technology.

All of this is to say that for the people we spoke to, questions about state of mind, culture and political will have to be answered before even contemplating the size of a country's administration. In 2015, the think tank *Renaissance Numérique* published a memo about Estonia, which highlighted the strengths of the Estonian model. One of them was the training of political decision-makers and senior civil servants, notably by giving them classes in design thinking, which gave them a better understanding of citizens' expectations and helped them make administrative services more accessible. Philippe Régnard, then Head of Institutional Relations for the Groupe La Poste, coordinated the writing of this memo, along with other members of the working group, and for him, "the Estonian example reaffirms the importance of an inclusive public policy. Beyond the necessary deployment of the infrastructure of very high-speed internet access, it's also about getting every citizen acclimated to digital technology, including and especially the elites, within a framework of trust, which allows for the development of digital functions. One of our first suggestions would be to replace our elites with Estonian digital elites! In Estonia, there is a specific category of "digital" senior civil servant, who graduated from the Tallinn University of Technology or an American university, MIT, etc. These 1,000 "digital"

---

13. Interview with the authors.

civil servants (out of 28,000) manage all the mechanics of X-Road, like the digital ID card and e-Residency."

France has had its own digital ambitions, including the development of an electronic ID card, but none of these have been successful, largely due to problems related to data confidentiality or a lack of political will. In order for the electronic ID card to make sense, it would have to be embedded within a system where citizens would have access to all services, as well as control over how their personal data was used (as is the case in Estonia). France might still be strongly incentivised to create this tool, because of European pressure.

Launched in 2013, the European project STORK2 (the follow-up to STORK) aims to "help create a single European space for electronic identification and authentication, enabling interoperability of electronic identification systems at the national and European levels, for legal and natural people".

France still has a long way to go. FranceConnect, a programme that allows people to use a single username when accessing multiple State services, was launched in 2016. Another programme, *Dites-le nous une fois* [Tell us once], was launched in 2013, and is supposed to be closer to the Estonian principle of never asking a citizen for the same information twice. Users' data now circulate more easily between administrations, limiting duplication of information and preventing users from having to provide documents that were already submitted for another file. This programme's first objective is making sure that companies only have to provide identification, social and accounting data once, along with any proof already provided elsewhere. This means that businesses only have to submit their SIRET code (which provides geographic identification for French establishments and businesses) when completing any administrative steps, and companies only have to transmit information regarding their revenue, employees and all fiscal and social data, once. However, these examples of progress are far cries from establishing a holistic approach to how citizens relate to digital technology.

When Urve Palo, the former Estonian Minister of Entrepreneurship and Information Technology, visited Paris on March 18, 2018, she signed a cooperative agreement with the former French Secretary of State for Digital Affairs, Mounir Mahjoubi. Let's hope that this will help France take even greater inspiration from the Estonian example. Without a digital ID card that's obligatory for everyone, without a heavily encrypted electronic signature that's obligatory for everyone and especially without a kind of X-Road that guarantees interoperability between all services, no decisive progress will ever be made. Small steps will not build a system that's transparent for citizens. So, let's listen to the Estonians and let's believe in the large-scale adaptability of their model. However, let's not forget that the space given to citizens is key to this model being able to function.

In Estonia, citizens hold a very important position: they're the clients that the State works to serve, to the best of its capabilities. The State is in the service of its citizens. In France however, civil servants follow in the tradition of serving the State, which conceives of and delivers services to its users. The ability to transpose the Estonian model on a larger scale does not depend on the number of inhabitants, the size of the country, its history, or the technologies that need to be implemented: instead, it relies on the very notion of the State and its relationship to its citizens. In this context, we can see that this isn't just a matter of a single project, but rather, a true political programme, a cultural revolution which aims to place citizens' interests first and to use innovation to consistently serve them better, by making their daily lives easier.

This makes all the difference between the idea of the common good, as personified by citizens, and that of public interest, which is intangible and which in France, has been effectively pre-empted by high-ranking civil servants for many years.

7. Estonian Paradoxes

Estonia can be seen as a model for entrepreneurship and the digital State. However, this doesn't include all of the complexities of this country, which has its own difficulties and paradoxes.

Estonian democracy: strengths and weaknesses

Estonia has a much more positive relationship with democracy than other former Eastern bloc countries. According to a poll conducted by the think tank Fondapol (Foundation Innovation Policy) and IPSOS, under the supervision of Dominique Reynié, entitled *Où va la démocratie* [Where is democracy going], only 41% of Estonians think that democracy works badly, versus 37% in Sweden, 53% in France, 59% in Poland and 66% in Latvia.

To the question, "Is the democratic system irreplaceable?", 64% of Estonians responded "Yes": 84% said yes in the Nordic countries, as opposed to only 49% in Latvia and 42% in Slovakia. When asked about the usefulness of voting, Estonia was far closer to Finland than to the other Baltic countries.

In *Fragile démocratie à l'Est* [Fragile democracy in the East][1], Corinne Deloy comments, "If the principle of democracy is voted in by respondents, they don't seem entirely satisfied with how it functions, except in Estonia. [...] With the notable exception of Estonians, the majority of people questioned spoke about their dissatisfaction with their government and Parliament."

There is a strong attachment to economic liberalism in Estonia. "Limit the role of the State and leave businesses alone" won the approval of 73% of Estonians, for a European average of 61%. Trust in small and medium size businesses (SMBs), 82%, is also higher than the average (69%), as well as the trust in large companies, which is 66%, as opposed to an average of 37%.

This powerful support of democracy does not, however, translate into high rates of participation in different elections, despite the establishment of an electronic voting system. For Geoffroy Berson[2], "the life of an Estonian citizen is certainly far simpler than it would be elsewhere. The use of online services, which only requires a few seconds or minutes each time, has fully entered daily life and allows people to enjoy an easy relationship with their administration. It's the same with politics, where the electronic

---

1. Fondapol.org

2. Former Attaché for Cooperation on Digital Innovation at the French Institute of Estonia in Tallinn.

vote affects close to one out of three voters at each election, and which arouses regular debate, but is never directly questioned."

Electronic voting isn't the only tool being used to increase voter participation: polling stations have been installed in strategic locations like shopping centres, absentee voting has been implemented, and the voting period is quite long.

Despite all of this, participation rates are only slightly higher than in neighbouring countries and in 2017, reached 55% in the local elections. The Estonian parliamentary elections in March 2019 saw a higher voter turnout, with 63.7%, but the European Parliament elections that followed two months later had a voter turnout of only 37.6%.Therefore, even though how the State functions is supposed to exemplify a model wherein it serves its citizens through trust and transparency, electoral participation doesn't reflect this. Clearly, the many reasons for this are convoluted and run the gamut from the complexity of the electoral system to the flaws of the political class. Nonetheless, it remains an inconsistency in a Nation that prides itself on how it relates to its citizens.

Another paradox was discovered by researchers at the Tallinn University of Technology: "The development of these public digital infrastructures, and especially of i-Voting, has not led to the emergence of a real 'digital democracy'.

This means that these digital tools do not allow citizens to have greater power over political decisions or how the State functions. When it comes to their relationship with public authorities, Estonian citizens are no more proactive than French citizens."

Geoffroy Berson's[3] analysis of the relationships between the State as a platform, the citizen, and civic tech in Estonia sheds an interesting light on how digital democracy has been developed: "X-Road, with the different e-Services built around it, is the result of a kind of vast public-private partnership. It's effective in its capacity to make companies and administrations collaborate, but its services which are dedicated to citizens and to the democratic are not central to it. Taavi Kotka, the first CIO of the Estonian government, who was in office until 2017, was frank on how he didn't believe in the hype surrounding open data or the claims of civic tech. For him, the only thing that really mattered was how technically efficient an online service was, a point of view that sees the citizen as a mere consumer."

This does not mean that Estonian civic tech doesn't exist. In fact, it has been around for a while: in 2001, the government opened a platform to collect the opinions of citizens. It was one of the first initiatives of its kind in the world! It was also far too ahead of its time and ended up being a failure.

Today, the main civic tech tool is called rahvaalgatus.ee ("the initiative of the people"). It's a site for petitions, which we've seen in other countries, except that this one leans on Estonia's main asset: its digital infrastructure. The signatures on the site are authenticated when citizens use their digital ID cards, so each petition is legitimate. Parliament has committed to recording every proposition that has garnered

---

3.   Former Attaché for Cooperation on Digital Innovation at the French Institute of Estonia in Tallinn.

more than 1,000 supporting votes. In two years, three laws have been passed through this process, but the tool has barely made a dent in daily life. A lot of thought has been given as to how to reinforce its impact on the country's political situation.

From a civil society perspective, local civic tech activists are very creative and are buzzing with projects: a platform where political decisions are made visual, a tracking tool for coalition government engagements, etc. They don't, however, always have the means to follow through on their ambitions. Nonetheless, they're being listened to more receptively by Estonian officials, which might pave the way for new innovations.

However, a real sense of the common good and a government that places citizens in a central role don't make the citizens any less of individuals. This is because of Estonian introversion, combined with a reactionary attitude towards anything reminiscent of Soviet-era collectivism. This is what Frédérico Planta, former employee of e-Estonia Showroom told Luca Minisini in his article "La vraie start-up nation" [The true start-up nation][4]: "This idea of managing a State like a business, it's like Estonia's post-traumatic stress reaction to Communism. People didn't have any freedom, so now, they do what they want and they don't care." Circumstances that aren't always favourable to developing shared reflection on the common good.

---

4.   *Society*, April 19, 2018.

A nation of the old where the young have power

The demographics of the Estonian population make its political leaders worry. Each year, the country loses 10,000 inhabitants and has 10,000 more retirees. This is a cause for concern because with a fertility rate of 1.6 children per woman, if no effective measures are put in place, it's the very future of the Estonian nation that's at stake. This also ties into something we noticed when we met the ambassadors of e-Estonia in Tallinn: they were mostly young (in their 30s) and childless.

In conversation, the situation sounds simple: yes, pensions are low, but family solidarity, coupled with the current economic success, means that the most elderly will be provided for. And yet, we're seeing more and more retirees who have to go back to work, or are living alone and in poverty. Family solidarity can't be the only response.

The idea that there's a lack of wealth redistribution is starting to spread politically and the government has just introduced a more progressive income tax policy, which up until now was based on a flat tax. The shortage in the labour force has made it so that no one is paid a minimum wage.

The salary of an unqualified labourer is around €700. For retirees, the average pension is €500. The average salary is €1,200.[5]

---

5.   Estonian Ministry of Economic Affairs.

Within the e-Nation, the relationship to the elderly is an ambivalent one: the Tiger Leap policy brought special attention to senior citizens, with the setting up of computers in libraries, along with training sessions, and in buses that travelled to the most remote villages. But the assumption was that young people would train them, and the measures taken were often more coercive than incentivizing. Starting in 2009, retirement pension payments were done uniquely online, which without a doubt also contributed to the rising use of online banking services among the elderly. Familial support played an important role here: it was often young people who taught older people how to use a computer, especially children and grandchildren.

Questions about the aging population were joined by the phenomenon of expatriation. The brain drain was significant and the government did not succeed in curbing it: its response programme resulted in the return of only about a dozen people. For qualified profiles, salaries are a lot more attractive in the United States. For blue-collar workers, salaries for the same jobs are more competitive in Finland. Expatriation concerns every layer of society. This situation is the same as that in many other countries that joined the EU in or after 2004,like Lithuania, Bulgaria and Croatia. Despite the differences in political and economic situations, the rate of expatriation, especially in the direction of western countries, is higher here. Brexit might change that, but it remains a subject which merits further investigation on the European level...

For all that, despite the troubling demographics, Estonians are ambivalent about different types of migration. Is this, as Ivan Krastev[6] contends, the double consequence of a State that doesn't want to risk disappearing once again into a much larger, multinational Empire but that was also built on cultural and linguistic homogeneity? Estonia has a significant rate of migrants who leave after they've entered, which can easily be chalked up to difficulties with the language.

A society where progress doesn't involve everyone

The economist Karsten Staehr recently told Lucas Minisini when he was sent to Tallinn to report for *Society* magazine, "In Estonia, there's team A, the winners of digitisation, then there's team B, the losers." In the same article, Thomas Padovani, investor and founder of Adcash, married to an Estonian, confirmed the existence of this gap: "My mother-in-law is a nurse. And a few years ago, she earned only €480 a month, which is not much when you look at the cost of living here. So, is Estonia a perfect country? The answer is no."

We can only note that the expansion of the economy's service sector hasn't benefited everyone and has even marginalised a part of the population. In fact, Estonia is unlikely to reach Finland's 85% standard

---

6. *After Europe*, Ivan Krastev, Penn University Press, 2017.

of living for another 15 years[7]. This marginalisation helps explain the results of the last legislative elections and the increase in the populist vote, with the Conservative People's Party of Estonia (EKRE) taking 19 parliamentary seats. While the Estonian Reform Party had been in the lead, it was unable to form a coalition, and now the EKRE is part of the current government coalition.[8]

Estonia is also facing a drug problem, namely the consumption of a synthetic opioid called Fentanyl, which is 50%-100% more powerful than morphine and which is why Estonia tops the EU drug overdose death list. The HIV rate remains high, even if it dropped by two-thirds between 2007 and 2016. By 2015 however, there were still 20 new cases for every 100,000 people, or three times more than the EU average, which is 5.8 new cases.[9] There is still room for progress when it comes to healthcare policy.

While elderly people, with their low pensions (a holdover from Soviet times) are clearly among those who are excluded in the population, they're not the only ones. The Russian-speaking minority has a much lower rate of education, a much higher rate of unemployment, lower incomes and more alarming health indicators (drugs and HIV, for example) than the Estonian-speaking majority. The Russian-speaking

---

7. GDP per inhabitant in 2017: In Estonia: €18,977. In France: €42,567. In Finland: €47,057. (Source: Trading economics)

8. On April 17, 2019, Parliament approved a coalition between the centrist political party, Isamaa, and EKRE. Jüri Ratas's second cabinet came into office on April 29, 2019. Each of the three parties in the coalition has five ministers in the cabinet.

9. UNAIDS

minority makes up over 25% of the population and has become more visible over the last 10 years, thanks in particular to the growing number of politicians representing it.

For Siim Kallas (Prime Minster of Estonia from 2002 to 2003 and EU Commissioner from 2004 to 2010), Russian-speakers who make the effort to learn Estonian integrate and find work. It's true that Estonia has implemented a policy that respects the rights of this minority, following European standards. The fact remains however that this minority is still missing within the Estonian model and from among the ranks of its architects. It's no accident that the Centre Party, which represents Estonia's Russian-speakers, is the political party that's the most vocal about favouring greater redistribution: Russian speakers have long been left by the wayside. Social exclusion, language barriers, the lack of a solid societal safety net, weak levels of education, low quality of life, a high rate of criminality...the list of grievances for Russian-speakers living in Estonia is similar to that of any excluded and dispossessed minority group.

The biggest gender pay gap in Europe

Another paradox: diversity. Estonian women were granted the right to vote in 1918 and its current president is a woman.

At 49, Kersti Kaljulaid is the youngest president of Estonia and its first female president. A marathon runner, who often participates in athletic competitions[10], with a degree in genetics and an MBA, she spent a great deal of her career as Estonia's representative in the European Court of Auditors, before being elected by the Estonian electoral assembly in 2016.

Many women have broken the glass ceiling in multiple areas, including the president and several ambassadors. Arnaud Castaignet[11] has noted the relative egalitarianism of the Estonian tech environment. The NGO TechSisters is developing initiatives to attract more women to the tech industry. "Over 40% of the people who lead companies in these industries are women in Estonia. France, with its 10% of start ups founded by women, pales in comparison."[12]

"The perspective on women has changed," confirms Mari Vavulski, head of Startup Estonia, a government organisation, which looks to boost the country's start up ecosystem. "Now, they're some of the Web entrepreneurs who lead economic rankings," writes Delphine Bauer in an article published in *Madame Figaro*, on January 14, 2018. On the European level, only 14.7% of European tech unicorns were founded by women, as opposed to 17% in the United States.

10. "President Kersti Kaljulaid participated in the 29th Étape du Tour de France on Sunday [July 21, 2019], a public stage of the men's annual multistage bicycle race…[she completed] a 135-kilometer route that included a total of 4,563 meters in climbs en route from Albertsville to Val Thorens. The stage concluded 2,365 meters above sea level, a record high stage finish line elevation in the Tour de France.", *ERR.ee*, July 22, 2019.

11. Former Head of Public Relations for the e-Residency programme.

12. *Madame Figaro*, January 14, 2018.

Among the most talked about women start uppers, we find Karoli Hindriks, 34 years old and CEO of Jobbatical (ranked by *Forbes* as one of the most promising companies to watch). Another key figure is Kaidi Ruusalepp, the founder of Funderbeam. She became the first lawyer in Estonia to specialise in IT in the 1990s and she was working in the Prime Minister's cabinet before she had a degree. She co-founded the NASDAQ OMX Tallinn (the Tallinn Stock Exchange), before creating her start up while on maternity leave, and was just named Entrepreneur of the Year in 2018 by the Technology Playmaker Awards. Kristel Kruustük is 28 years old, looks like a rock star and is a product of the Tiger Leap programme, which the government launched in 1996 to facilitate internet access in schools. As a testing officer, she won the AngelHackhackathon in London in 2012, and then founded Testlio, where she's CEO, along with now-husband Marko Kruustük. Microsoft, Lyft and the NBA are just some of their clients, and Testlio has raised $6 million in funds.[13]

Despite these impressive figures, Estonia holds the record for the worst gender pay gap in Europe[14], which rose to 25.3% in 2016: compare this to 16.2% in the eurozone and 15% in France.[15] In a country that is so modern in some areas, women still play background roles in many fields. And yet, we can't

13. *Madame Figaro*, January 14, 2018.

14. eer.ee

15. Eurostat.

say it's because they're having children (never mind the fact that the traditional mindset is even worse)!

Estonia provides the longest paid maternity leave in the OECD (435 days) and women receive 100% of the average salary they were earning in the year prior to their maternity leave. The same conditions apply to paternity leave, although only one parent can take advantage of these benefits. The length of time granted partly explains why a lot of women end up leaving the working world. Outside of tech, they are the most likely to take on jobs that require unskilled labour. Kristjan Vassil, a researcher who specialises in the impact of new technologies, thinks that data could help improve the situation. In his own words, "information about the remunerative gap between the sexes can be reviewed in real time, with the help of data collected from tax and customs boards declarations, which wouldn't directly compromise anyone's interests. We've set policy objectives that we want to achieve, but we haven't determined any tangible measurements for how we'll monitor our progress. These kinds of real-time economic dashboards would allow us to go as deeply into specific performance indicators as we'd like: with digital solutions, we'd be able to achieve equality at a societal level."[16]

For the Estonian President, "This is certainly an issue that we must deal with. The pay gap and domestic violence are on going issues. Typically, a regular citizen might deny that these things exist or even make a joke about them. The parliament jokes

---

16. "On the next generation of public e-services", site: e-Estonia, March 2018.

about it and still asks questions like, 'Why aren't there enough Estonian women for Estonian men?' Sorry, but education and the work that goes with it will take us some more time.

Fortunately, more and more, this is not a problem for young people. Also, if we look at how work life has changed, we see that the work day is no longer always from 9 AM to 5 PM, Monday to Friday, and this will also reduce the pay gap, because more flexible work hours will allow men and women to better coordinate family life."[17]

According to the OECD, Estonia is the third most homophobic country in the organisation, after Turkey and Latvia.[18] Same-sex couples have been allowed to sign cohabitation agreements since January 1, 2016, but Estonia is also one of 16 countries in the OECD where gay marriage is prohibited, while 19 OECD countries allow it, based on data from 2017.

The societal component is very important: "To achieve a more inclusive society, Estonia should combat discrimination and abuses against older people, tackle the gender pay gap and violence against women, and devote more efforts to building social cohesion," declared Dunja Mijatovi, the Council of Europe Commissioner for Human Rights, after a five-day visit to Estonia.[19]

---

17. "A small country has only one natural resource – between our ears", Kersti Kaljulaid, *Estonian World*, February 24, 2017, published in 2018.

18. "Estonia is one of the most homophobic countries in the OECD", *Estonian world*, May 2018.

19. "European human rights authority: Estonia needs more social cohesion", *Estonian world*, June 2018.

The environment

Chantal de Bourmont, former French Ambassador to Estonia, was very impressed by how close Estonians were to nature. Estonia is one of the least religious countries in the world, with only 16% of the population saying that religion has any importance in their lives. At the same time, 69% believe that trees have souls.[20] At the heart of this subject is a proposal for a high-speed, trans-Baltic railway line, which was rejected because there was a risk it would disturb the movement of animals.

"In one sense, environmental issues concerning the railway are actually easy to solve. It turns out that in some places, bridges cannot be built with an incline slight enough so that elk can cross, because they do not climb over hills. But you can build the railway over the hill and let the elk cross underneath. These are all the issues that can be resolved when we focus on how to get it done, instead of denying the project," explained President Kersti Kaljulaid.[21]

And yet, ecology comes second to the necessity of independence, especially when talking about energy, which is mostly drawn from highly polluting oil shales. Another paradox for these nature lovers is that Estonia has more cars per inhabitant than the United States, which is of course because of the climate, but is also a testament to their individualist characters.

---

20. *Estonian World.*

21. "A small country has only one natural resource – between our ears", Kersti Kaljulaid, *Estonian World*, February 24, 2017, published in 2018.

In order to encourage greater use of public transportation, the free transport that was already in place for Tallinn inhabitants was extended to the rest of the country in July 2018. Free transport is exclusively on public county bus lines, thanks to an increase in government subsidies for regional transport organisations, which cover any losses in ticket fares. Bus lines in cities outside of Tallinn, like trains, still charge fares.[22] There are also a large number of high performing start ups and companies within the sustainable development sector, including the wood industry, where Estonia is the primary European exporter.

At the last Tallinn Digital Summit in September 2019, 33 Estonian technology companies signed a "green pledge", promising to take their operations to a completely environmentally sustainable basis by 2030[23]. With this Green Pledge, the Estonian technology sector is prioritising the environment as an integral part of their business.

Cultural paradoxes, diversity, social issues: there's still a lot of work to be done if Estonia doesn't want to have a two-tier society. Of course, this young country still has significant demographic, societal and cultural challenges to face, but let's not forget, Rome wasn't built in a day, and while it took Estonia less than 25 years to become a digital technology pioneer, it's still a very young State.

22. *Le Figaro*, June 5, 2018.
23. "Over 30 Estonian tech companies sign a green pledge to become climate neutral", *Estonian World*, September 17, 2019.

8. Estonia's European Issues

Geopolitics led by allying with Europe in the face of Russia

Like several other member countries, Estonia's geo-political system has been marked by its complicated relationship with Russia.

For Estonians, a TV series like *Occupied*[1], which tells the story of a Russian invasion of Norway, doesn't feel like fiction, but instead, taps into a real fear that also explains Estonia's feelings of solidarity with Ukraine. Estonia has always had a border conflict with Russia. Trade relations also took a nosedive after Russia's retaliatory measures in the wake of European sanctions (notably on apples and dairy products). As Erkki Bahovski, editor-in-chief of the magazine *Diplomaatia*, puts it, "Russia knows how to switch between *The Godfather* and *The Sound of Music* when it comes to appearances, but the only real Russia is *The Godfather*." Faced with this Russian threat, Estonia's decision to join both NATO and the EU in 2004 seems

---

1. TV2, 2015.

like a way to shield itself, an attempt to guarantee its safety. NATO is very present in Estonia, with a military base and the NATO Cyber Defence Centre of Excellence in Tallinn.

The president of Estonia recently reiterated her country's attachment to the North Atlantic Treaty Organisation: "We need NATO. Does the EU work? The answer has always been, 'It has problems but it's the best option we've got'. And it's exactly the same thing with NATO. It's the best system that we have. It's the only one that protects all of us right now." [2]

For many Estonians, the EU is the antithesis of the USSR. As former Prime Minister Siim Kallas explains, "I remember how the Soviet Union hated Europe, because Europe, it was voluntary, while the USSR was an empire."

This alliance with Europe and NATO is of extreme importance for all Estonians. The Centre Party, which was voted in by Estonian Russian-speakers, and which has a cooperative agreement with Russia and Vladimir Putin, would have had to publicly deny any attachment to NATO and the EU before it could put together the coalition that's currently in power.

In an article from July 2, 2018[3], Matthew Crawdall highlights the challenge American withdrawal poses for small States. He takes Estonia as an example of success: "Estonia has developed a niche strategy as a

2. Interview with President Kersti Kajulaid, "Il faut parler avec la Russie, mais sans naïveté" [We must talk to Russia, but we mustn't be naive about it], France 24, November 18, 2019.

3. "The era of Trump means it is time for small States to start thinking big", *Euronews*, July 2, 2018.

cyber expert." He also notes that the country, although very much an Atlanticist, knew not to put all its eggs into one basket, for example when supporting French operations in Africa. For him, Estonians have chosen to invest in a "multi-vector foreign policy", even as he notes their insufficient efforts when it comes to major powers like India or Brazil.

Wanting to set itself apart from other Baltic countries

The three Baltic States are very different in terms of history, culture, religion and language, but also in standards of living and budgets. Lithuania has the same budget as Estonia but it has over twice the number of inhabitants. Estonia's social security budget is double that of Lithuania's.[4]

Of course, there are similarities, like the significance of their relationships with Russia, even if the way the Russian question is asked depends on the proportions of Russian-speakers in each country (only 6% in Lithuania, 25% in Estonia, 28% in Latvia).[5]Agreements between these States, revolving around defence, but also culture and tourism, have increased in the last few years. Nonetheless, ever since the country regained its independence, Estonia has yearned to stand out from its Baltic neighbours. Toomas Hendrik Ilves, former president of Estonia, recalls: "My goal was to separate Estonia from the

4.   Eurostat.

5.   Eurostat.

Baltic countries", to become "one more boring Nordic country".

From the beginning, Estonia did not want its UN seat to be in the Eastern European Group and this wish was granted—for all the Baltic countries, which are now grouped with the Nordic countries. In an article entitled *Have we become Swedish?*[6], a Lithuanian journalist questioned the fact that the UN placed the three Baltic countries in the same category as the Nordic nations. This seemed strange to him, given the significant differences between a country like Lithuania and the Nordic countries, but also revealing of the difficulties that exist in separating the three Baltic States.

From the moment Estonia drew closer to the Nordic countries, the three Baltic nations have been seen in the same light. For the former French ambassador, Chantal de Bourmont, this desire to be considered a northern country is an essential part of how Estonians defend their independence, culture, language and even their very existence.

Does digital technology mean a place in the EU?

For Estonia, it's not just about being a member of the EU, but of being recognised within this entity. To achieve this, digital technology represents the best and most exportable of Estonian expertise, so it made sense that when Estonia held its first presidency of the Council of the European Union, in the

6. *IQ Intelligent Life*, Vilnius, January 29, 2018.

second half of 2017, it used this position to emphasise digital issues.

The Estonian presidency had a multifaceted approach to digital technology, which touches on all areas because it involves data. From this perspective, Estonia highlighted the single market strategy for dealing with data, hoping to make the free movement of data the fifth fundamental freedom (after the free movement of people and money, and the exchange of services and goods). The country was very active during its presidency, organising "over 275 events and leading more than 1,200 task forces in Brussels".[7] Estonia also built up its legitimacy by using its own example as a platform for its presidency: "The Estonian presidency made good use of one of the political resources available to it: positive talk grounded in its national expertise, the digital."[8]

The overall Estonian strategy relied on the Estonian presence in Brussels: the European Commissioner for Digital Single Market (Andrus Ansip[9]) and the six Estonian Members of the European Parliament, notably those of RENEW (formerly known as the Alliance of Liberals and Democrats for Europe Party, or ALDE), were very active from 2014 to 2019. Whether it was Ansip talking about the "digital revolution" and the "digital era" or former Member of the European

---

7. Bilan numérique de la présidence estonienne [Digital assessment of the Estonian presidency], Clément Harmegnies, *Le Taurillon*, February 16, 2018.

8. Ibid.

9. Former Prime Minister and Commissioner, elected to be a Member of the European Parliament in May 2019.

Parliament, Kaja Kallas[10], saying that she "hopes to show the rest of Europe that digital transformation is good progress", a positive outlook towards the digital was on the rise. It was of note that the EU was considered by Andrus Ansip to be the most relevant actor; he insisted on the fact that, "the European Union must become a leader in terms of [digital] innovation".

For the Estonian presidency, the values of cyberspace had to be supported by liberal democracy. Clément Harmegnies emphasised that, "within the framework of cyber-democracy and its channel of online administration, Estonia preserves the values of freedom, responsibility, trust, transparency, innovation and personal safety."

"It's important to note that, for the first time in its history, the European Council has had at its head a leader in the digital realm, even if it's also important to remember that the Estonian enthusiasm for the digital isn't shared by all of the member countries, as certain States show themselves to be culturally more fearful, and others don't consider the digital to be a priority."

More concretely, here were the subjects addressed by the Estonian presidency: it wanted to push as far as possible the principle of free movement within a single digital market, including data, so as to contribute to creating an ecosystem that permitted revolutionary innovations; it also insisted on the importance of standardising laws in order to accelerate growth.

---

10. Reform Party Chairwoman

In terms of the interoperability of data and digital technologies, it invested a great deal in cooperation agreements on using low-frequency bands for 5G networks and putting an end to unjustified geo-blocking for the use of content, as well as royalty reforms in a digital context.

During its presidency, Estonia also insisted on the necessity of adopting the e-ID (the digital ID card) in all European countries, and emphasised its expertise in cybersecurity, which led to the passing of the first European law on cybersecurity in 2018. Estonia also brought to the other countries' attention its X-Road technology and blockchain technology as a whole. Following the Estonian presidency, on February 1, 2018, the European Commission launched the EU Blockchain Observatory and Forum, with the aim of encouraging European governments, businesses and citizens to take advantage of the possibilities offered by this technology. Its time as president allowed Estonia to promote its vision of an inclusive digital society that would be fully integrated into the social model, which wouldn't leave any citizen behind and which wouldn't neglect important issues like education, training and the mastering of digital knowledge.

The Tallinn Digital Summit of September 29, 2017 was the occasion for a shared declaration that touched on the main points held up by the Estonian presidency: e-Government and cybersecurity; blockchain technology; the digital data market and the necessity of not being opposed to disruptive technologies and of facilitating the movement of data; digital education; and inclusive digital technology.

It also addressed the taxation of multinational companies by highlighting the need to maintain room for manoeuvre, while simultaneously avoiding entering into unjust practices.

Beyond this presidency, there's another critical area where Estonia can bring added value to the entirety of the EU: interoperability. In fact, e-Government has become a border-crossing issue.

The interoperability between Estonia and Finland is a good example of what the EU's future with interoperable public services could hold. It's true of course that these two countries are already deeply connected with a living cooperation in terms of economics, trade and culture, a transnational labour force and a shared X-road infrastructure for their public services, which Estonia convinced Finland to adopt. However, the 2017 decision to share a data exchange system for the public sector was still a bold one and the cooperation is social, financial and also health care-related. As Linnar Viik, founder and director of the Estonian e-Governance Academy and Programme recalls[11]: "With Finland, we connected social security operations, the tax, work and certifications bureaus, and the health platforms. So for example, doctors' diagnoses and prescriptions are recognised and used digitally by Estonians and Finns in both countries."

Imagine a Swiss doctor being able to instantaneously access the medical files of a Hungarian patient, or an Italian company being able to digitally sign a contract with their British counterpart. This is the

---

11. *Life in Estonia*, February 2018.

future of the European Union. And Estonia, as a leader in the field, hopes that the transnational exchange of data will soon be possible between all European countries. The advantages for citizens are obvious, but there are many for companies as well, which should contribute to the realising of a single market.

"Today's greatest challenges are not linked to Estonia and the Estonian e-Government. The biggest challenge is the fact that we are not a self-sufficient nation, but a member of the European Union and the eurozone," explains Linnar Viik, founder and director of the Estonian e-Governance Academy. "We will not be able to find solutions that are only applicable to Estonia, while acting within the European Union. This is why our country is one of the most ardent defenders of the idea of free movement of data within a single market, and this is also why we must develop interoperability with other member States."[12]

During a study trip in October 2017 that was co-organised by Digeetrips and the think tank Atelier Europe, we met Klen Jäärats, who was Director for European Union Affairs in the State Chancellery at the time. A rising star in Estonian politics, he's quickly being considered one of Europe's most influential spin doctors. With a colourfulness that calls to mind Winston Churchill, he spoke to us about many important topics.

"Estonia is a reliable and predictable partner, and it has always endeavoured to positively contribute to the future of Europe. Through the subjects addressed

---

12. *Life in Estonia*, February 2018.

during its presidency of the EU Council, Estonia suggested that the societal angle was the main issue of digital technology in Europe. In fact, with this in mind, the digital is less about technology (telcos or 5G) than it is about what we can do with it. Digital technology is useful both for what it allows us to do and how it allows us to reduce costs."

In the realm of digital technology, Europe failed the platform revolution and has fallen behind the big tech countries: the United States, China and Singapore. According to Klen Jäärats, the next European challenge will involve artificial intelligence, which will require greater efforts in cybersecurity and the development of digital society. "It's especially for this reason that the Estonian presidency wanted to push as much as possible the principle of free movement of data in Europe. The goal is to help create an ecosystem that allows revolutionary innovations, to help sparka 'Sputnik moment' like there was in the US when it responded to Soviet advances in technology and space with the creation of DARPA (the Defence Advanced Research Projects Agency). For that to happen, the standardisation of laws is paramount, so that companies like Blablacar can quickly expand to a wider scale."

The Director for European Affairs insists that we must change the ways we think about and write laws if we want to win the war of innovation. "European citizens need to trust digital technology in order to save Europe from losing the services that it produces. Blockchain technology, which relies on the principle of shared trust, is changing the way we think about public policy."

The challenges of the fourth Industrial Revolution reveal a number of issues: how do we introduce iteration into the establishment of laws? How do we quickly manage change? These questions are crucial because whichever country has managed to adjust the most will end up winning the global war of innovation.

For Estonians, it's obvious that their country plays an important role in the EU. After all, it's a member of the eurozone and the Schengen Area and it's far ahead of its European partners when it comes to e-Government for Estonians: to them, their country is ready for reinforced cooperation agreements with the big States, it's part of a close circle. It's less clear whether or not western European political leaders, who brought the idea of a "Europe of concentric circles" back into fashion, also think of distant, little Estonia as part of that circle...

Many European countries, and especially France, still have a vision of Europe that's quite uneven. They very rarely turn their gaze to the East, and even less frequently to the "small" countries. And yet, as President Kersti Kaljulaid said in an interview with *The Wall Street Journal*[13], "How do we know where the next big innovation will come from? From Georgia? Or Ukraine?" Today, investment in innovation per inhabitant in Estonia is close to double that of

13. The Baltic States Turn 100, One lesson we have learned is that the benefits of freedom can be wide-ranging and unpredictable. Kersti Kaljulaid *The Wall Street Journal*, February 7, 2018.

France.[14] Estonia, along with Slovenia, which does a lot of work in cybersecurity, are the two most developed digital markets.

But there's also Fintech and software in the Czech Republic, Romania, Lithuania and Poland, and there's gaming in Latvia and Bulgaria. We're going to have to start looking differently at the Europeans countries that have changed the way we think about digital technology and which has more surprises in store for us.

In Estonia, but also in certain eastern and central European countries, there's been a very positive and hopeful response to the many visits from French leaders, as well as the presence of French President Emmanuel Macron, who often expresses his interest in different national situations. He seems to represent a Europe, led by certain large countries, that no longer overlooks the member countries to the East and the North, which have become wonderful breeding grounds of innovation!

---

14. Per capita investment in innovation: Estonia, $60; France, $33; the United States, $185. *East-West Digital News*, December 2017.

9. The Future in Estonia

"Creating the future now is the driving project of Estonia and increasingly, its core business," declared Ahti Heinla, the founding developer of Skype and co-founder of Starship Technology, a robotic delivery vehicle start up.[1]

The country is maintaining its dynamism and spirit of innovation by embracing the digital revolution. Halfway between a fab lab and a think tank, "What's next?" could easily be Estonia's motto. In the last 25 years' worth of projects conducted in Estonia, we can see the beginnings of an Estonian method. The development of biobanks is just one example.

Genomics

The Estonian Biobank is the Estonian Genome Centre's biobank, located at the University of Tartu. Created in 2000, its goal is to take DNA samples from a quarter of the country's population. Estonia's small

---

1. *Life in Estonia.*

size and relatively homogeneous population make it an ideal place for implementing the ambitious idea of DNA sequencing a population.

The goal of this genome sequencing project is to develop personalised and preventative medicine within the national health care system. "Today, Estonia has about 70,000 diabetics—if we could help even one-fifth of them, that would be a great number. We have 28,000 people who have gone blind from glaucoma, but in 90% of the cases, it is a form of the disease where the possibilities of genetics could be applied and people could be sent early for monitoring and have their intraocular pressure measured. Breast cancer is another disease where we could identify people who should undergo early screening," says Professor Andres Metspalu, director of the biobank and Genome Centre and professor of biology at the University of Tartu.[2] "The Estonian government wants to develop its health care system by offering all residents genome-wide genotyping, to be used in daily medical practice via the national e-Health portal," stated the Minister of Social Affairs in a report that was released at the start of April 2018.

Professor Metspalu believes that the predictive power of genetic data will allow the Estonian health-care system to go from a reactive to a preventative system. "Today, we treat patients. But we should be able to keep them in good health. When a person knows their personal genetic tendencies, that can motivate them to adopt a healthy way of life."[3]

---

2.   Connectedhealth.ee, July 2017.

3.   e-Health cluster.

For Ain Aaviksoo, former Under Secretary for e-Services and Innovation in Healthcare[4], "It's like basic education. The government provides the infrastructure, the people, the methods and the procedure, and everybody gets access to that. By and large, this is a system that is there to support you in the most important role, which is, behaving on behalf of your own health." He predicts a future in medicine where patients will be able to use all sorts of technologies—parsed genetic data, but also things like wearables—to play a larger and more important role in managing their health.[5]

This project follows the same methodology as that of others conducted in Estonia, made possible by deep political commitment and a favourable regulatory framework. The 1999 Estonian law on research involving human genes (the Estonian Human Genes Research Act), "is the cornerstone of the Estonian Biobank Project", says Andres Metspalu.[6] Within this framework, all participants sign a general statement of informed consent (www.biobank.ee). The law establishes anonymity in clinical research, enables donors to decide which studies they want to participate in, and gives them full control over who has access to their data. By default, a donor's doctor is the only other person who can look at their genetic information through the portal, unless the donor authorises more people. Transparency and citizens' trust are at

4.   Currently Chief medical officer at Guardtime Health
5.   "Estonia Wants to Collect the DNA of All Its Citizens", *The Atlantic*, October 8, 2015.
6.   Ibid.

the heart of the process, which explains the higher rate of support: in February 2002, only 13% of public opinion was in favour of the project, and in 2013, this number rose to 67%. The project's latest phase, launched in March 2018, puts greater emphasis on providing feedback for citizens who participate in the programme. Its aim is to have 25% of the population participate (as of today, only 5% have taken part).[7]

The biobank programme operates with the voluntary cooperation of doctors. During the first recruitment round, which lasted from 2002 to 2011, more than half of all Estonian medical professionals cooperated with the biobank, agreeing to integrate the process of donating into normal doctors' visits for those who were interested.[8] This association will expand in the years to come, according to Jevgeni Ossinovski, who was Minister of Health from 2015 to 2018: "Today, we have enough knowledge about both the genetic risk of complex diseases and the inter-individual variability of the effects of medicines, in order to begin systematically utilizing this information in everyday healthcare."[9]

---

7.   Ibid.

8.   Ibid.

9.   news.err.ee, March 2018.

How is this biobank doing so far? Has Estonia once again made itself an example?

There are currently over 120 biobanks in the world[10], but the majority of them focus on genomic research rather than personalised medicine. In Iceland, for example, biobanks are privately owned, so while around 40% of the country's population has given DNA for sequencing, this information hasn't been integrated into personal health on a national scale. The US also lacks the means to integrate large amounts of data from companies like 23andME into its health care system and Americans remain suspicious of how such companies are using their data. In fact, in June 2018, 23andME, which has genotyped more than one million customers, was accused of selling its customers' genetic data for profit.

In direct contrast, the Estonian biobanking system was built on a law that fundamentally protects the privacy of gene donors, while also establishing their rights.

By studying the genetic data of such an unvaried population, scientists can improve their understanding of hereditary diseases and the interaction of genetic and environmental factors. But the biobank also offers international researchers an extensive sample pool, which they can analyse by age, gender, education and lifestyle. MIT biology professor Eric Lander also believes that Estonia is a model of what

10. "Estonia Wants to Collect the DNA of All Its Citizens", *The Atlantic*, October 8, 2015.

the future might look like, despite its imperfections: "Think of the amazing opportunities that come from combining the IT infrastructure and the public trust in it with the information that can be learned from the genome," he said, during a 2014 talk at the University of Tartu. "There are so many opportunities to turn medicine into a learning system."[11]

The Estonian biobank has been a success, demonstrating the State's ability to invest in the future. Or, as Andres Metspalu cheekily puts it: "Portugal has wonderful motorways; we have a centre for genomic studies."[12] Estonia is investing in the future and displaying its own approach to predictive medicine that relies on genomes, which up until now, was a heavily American movement. Once again, we see here how the public sector can seize huge opportunities, which in many other countries would be taken on by the private sector, thus allowing it to guarantee the ethical, transparent and democratic use of data.

Artificial intelligence

There's a new student at the University of Tartu, the most famous university in Estonia: a robot named Pepper. The primary role of the humanoid robot, which originated in France and was built by the Japanese company SoftBank, is to keep people company. Pepper used to welcome guests to the Estonian

---

11. "Estonia Wants to Collect the DNA of All Its Citizens", *The Atlantic*, October 8, 2015.

12. Interview with the authors.

headquarters of the Nordic telecommunications company Telia, which also finances robot studies at the university. "If everything goes as planned, Pepper will obtain various skills and knowledge by the end of the semester, to communicate with people even better than before," the university announced on its website. Karl Kruusamäe, associate professor at the university and Pepper's supervisor, adds, "On the one hand, our students will teach Pepper how to communicate with people in an easily understandable manner in the physical world and in virtual reality. On the other hand, the students will learn through practical experience how to develop technologically highly complex robotic systems from predefined requirements."[13]

In 2017, Estonia officially authorised test runs of self-driving cars on the country's roads, provided there's a driver present who can take control if necessary. Self-driving shuttles are also being used on a trial basis in Tallinn over the summer.

Once again, we're talking about a skill that can be exported. Recently, teams from the French army went to Estonia to get robots from Milrem Robotics, an Estonian company. These robots will be put into operation in 2021 and will evacuate wounded soldiers, an operation that today requires two other soldiers to interrupt their missions to get it done.[14]

Robotics has invaded Estonia: robotic delivery vehicles, self-driving buses, specialty start ups... Broadly speaking, all of artificial intelligence has

13. *Estonian World*, April 16, 2018.

14. *La Tribune*, June 8, 2018.

become an important area of research expertise and a fully-fledged economic sector within digital technology.

Keeping this in mind, it's not surprising that Estonians are spearheading studies that look at the ethical and regulatory questions raised by artificial intelligence. Estonia aims to be the first country that passes laws in this area.

In a recent article, Peeter Meos, Data Science Lead, and Katariina Roosipuu, Marketing Lead, both at Proekspert, asked a fundamental question: "Would you entrust your life to artificial intelligence?"[15]

Artificial intelligence (AI) has created an entirely new range of ethical questions that challenge the very fabric of our society and threaten to undermine or make banal laws that have existed for hundreds, or even thousands, of years. The more we entrust key aspects of society and our daily lives to technology, the more we'll need to depend on it to make critical decisions about matters ranging from what track to play on the living room sound system, to whom we should save in a car crash.

"The favourite AI conundrum is the 'trolley problem'. In a crash, do you save the driver or the paying customer who bought the ticket? Is it acceptable for a product to decide to kill them both in order to save a child? Ethically, you should save the child, right? And how would the AI even know? There are too many factors at play: speed, intention, demographics and the culturally defined values of each individual. Because of problems like these, the industry is going through

---

15. e-Estonia.

a period of introspection. When engineering AI, you have no social mechanism: you have only robotic laws," write Peeter Meos and Katariina Roosipuu.

The Estonian government has been discussing a proposition that would grant certain rights to artificial intelligence systems, and help regulate decision-making by autonomous systems, robots and self-driving cars. This project has evolved since its conception, due to the complex changes that will need to be made to several laws in order to allow autonomous agents to operate and to grant them representative rights. These legislative proposals (which will also be applicable to self-driving cars) should be ready for Parliament by June 2020.

Marten Kaevats, National Digital Advisor of Estonia, led the planning of this law, which went by the name KrattLaw-Estonia. The *kratt* is a magical creature from Estonian mythology, a treasure-bearer created from an assembly of random objects that the Devil will bring to life for you, in exchange for a drop of blood, offered at the conjunction of five roads. The Devil gives the *kratt* a soul, making it the slave of its creator. This is why Marten Kaevats chose the name: his office spoke of the *kratt* instead of robots and algorithms and used the word to define a new, important nuance in Estonian law. "'Basically, a *kratt* is a robot with representative rights,'" he explains. "'The idea that an algorithm can buy and sell services on your behalf is a conceptual upgrade.' The digital shorthand of KrattLaw-Estonia for a new category of legal entity, comprising AI, algorithms and robots, will make it possible to hold accountable whoever gave a drop of blood. Such checks, device to device, have a distributed effect. To commandeer a self-driving car on the street, a saboteur would, in theory, also have to hack every street lamp and smart toaster it passed."[16]

Jaan Tallinn, founding engineer at Skype and Kazaa, has become a leading international expert in artificial intelligence. He is one of the founders of the Centre for the Study of Existential Risk at the University of Cambridge in the UK, as well as the Future of Life Institute in Cambridge, Massachusetts in the US. He's also an active investor in AIstart ups. In an interview given to the magazine, *Life in Estonia*, he returns to the big issues around artificial intelligence.[17] His first question is: "What will happen when our objectives and goals and the goals of super-intelligence do not align?"

According to him, the greatest short-term risk is that of democracy. But in the long term, it's the very survival of the human race. "We need to make it the goal of AI to sustain that narrow range of environmental parameters that enable continued biological life on the planet. By default, it wouldn't be in AI's interest, because it's not probable that the existence of atmosphere would suit the needs of AI." This is what he calls the existential threat and it's increased by the fact that the most powerful players in AI today are in the private sector.

---

16. *The New Yorker*, December 2017.

17. *Life in Estonia*, February 2018.

Jaan Tallinn concludes his interview with these words: "Welcome to the world of exponential growth. If you look at the history of world GDP over hundreds of years, you see that for a long time, nothing happens and then suddenly, everything happens. In a lot of spheres, the growth accelerates and it will be increasingly difficult for individuals to keep up with the pace."

AI in government: making administrative services invisible

The next step, as described by Siim Sikkut in his interview with *Under the Hood*[18], is to start making services invisible to citizens, so that with the help of AI, they will no longer have to engage in administrative tasks. "We operate on a 3-year roadmap horizon and we have a 2020 strategy which is based on the founding of the European Union's 7 years framework.

We are now starting to look at what the directions should be for 2021 and beyond. One thing to consider is automation with artificial intelligence. This is clearly a direction for us to take and the design of our digital services needs to take the transactional frontline services to the next level. Our goal is to have invisible services, which means that we can get rid of as many unnecessary interactions as we can. For example, if there is a new company in Estonia,

---

18. "Building the Digital Government – Estonia's Digital Transformation", *Under the Hood*, October 26, 2019.

all the reporting and all the red paper activities can be done online. Currently there are many individual transactions that have different webpages and different user experiences. We are now trying to look at it all holistically, which raises the question: do we need these at all? Why not have integration in company financial data; that way, all the reporting can be done automatically!

This is what we are building up in invisible services – machines exchanging data and 'talking' to each other. You, as an entrepreneur, would not need accountants to submit data and reports online. We can get rid of all that with automisation!

We will provide invisible services for citizens, too. For example, when your child is born, why do you need to go to 5 different websites to apply for things – let's integrate that into one website, and automate the entire process. In the first example, the government knows that the baby was born, because the hospital has already made an entry in the population registry. So, why do we wait for you to apply for basic things when we can initiate the interaction by sending an e-mail welcoming the baby, asking its name, asking what kindergarten you would like to send the baby to and what account we should send the money to? We ask you things we need to know to better serve you. These are the kind of things that we would like to bring in, creating a holistic life service and not just single silos and discrete transactions."

Giving the example of birth registries, Ott Velsberg, Chief Data Officer for the Ministry of Economic Affairs and Communications told ABC[19]: "'Why should the parent have to go and register that child for a kindergarten or apply for childcare funding and so on. All of this is done automatically.'

Mr Velsberg said 50 new AI government projects are scheduled to come online by next year, including satellite litter detection that will send automated messages to relative clean-up crews, and a robot judge that will further automate the small claims court system. Satellites are already being used to monitor farming projects, legal and illegal logging and ice detection in the Baltic Sea, which saves the Government over 1 million Euros ($1.6 million) and shipping companies 2 million ($3.3 million) per year."

Whether it be in terms of economics, e-Government, or ethics, Estonia has fully grasped the place that artificial intelligence will occupy in our future.

Cybersecurity and digital hygiene

Elected in 2016, President Kersti Kaljulaid emphasises Estonia's support of global digital security. On the opinions page of *The Wall Street Journal*, she recalls, "Estonia has transformed itself into a digital leader, creating the only digital society in the world, fully supported and protected in the cybersphere by the

---

19. "Estonia: From AI judges to robot bartenders, is the post-Soviet state the dark horse of digital tech?" ABC news, June 2019.

State. The world first heard of the digital Estonia in 2007, when the state came under cyberattack and had to fight back—a situation that could not have occurred in other countries at that point, simply because there was not enough to disrupt."[20]

Since then, Estonia has become the home of NATO's Cooperative Cyber Defence Centre of Excellence (CCDCOE), as well as the European Union Agency for the Operational Management of Large-Scale IT Systems. Estonia also hosts the annual International Conference on Cyber Conflicts (CyCon), which every year attracts 600 experts and decision-makers from the global cyberdefence community.

The CCDCOE organises the largest and most complex technical cyber defence exercise in the world, live, which in 2018, brought together 1,000 participants from 30 different countries. "In addition to solving technical challenges, it's important to understand the impact of cyberoperations at the strategic and political levels. This is what we're practising during the exercise," explains Merle Maigre, the fomer CCDCOE director[21].

2008 also saw the arrival of the Tallinn Manual process, which defined the foundations of international law within the context of cyber issues. Written by a group of experts appointed by NATO, the Tallinn Manual process transposes international law onto cyber conflicts. The first volume was published in 2013 and primarily examined military operations. The

---

20. *The Wall Street Journal*, February 7, 2018.

21. Now executive vice president at CybExer

second volume came out in 2016 and was written by a larger group of experts in order to take into account all cyberspace operations.

As President Kersti Kaljulaid explains, "You can create trust, but you have to create tools and the legal space that supports the security for these tools. The State has to promise people to keep them safe on the internet."[22]

The rise in cybercrimes and politically motivated attacks against electronic services proves that cybersecurity is more important than ever, both for the private and public sectors. Over the last decade, Estonia has grown significantly more prepared to face cyber emergencies. The country has created systems to detect and protect against intrusions, cooperated with public and private institutions, made critical contributions to raising awareness among users and continues to participate in an intensive international partnership.

The Estonian approach maintains the importance of digital hygiene or "cyber hygiene", one of the President's favourite topics. Estonia takes the attitude that even if you invest in the newest and most elaborate security systems, if the person using the software hasn't been properly trained and opens every single spam message, all of your investment means nothing.

This means that the most profitable way of ensuring cybersecurity is to train people individually, from students in schools to collaborators in companies.

---

22. From AI to Russia, Here's How Estonia's President Is Planning for the Future *Wired*, April 5, 2018.

The private and public sectors in Estonia have already started implementing this education. About a year ago, thousands of civil servants had to do an online test, which rated their knowledge of cyber hygiene. The test was created by the Estonian Ministry of Defence and the company CybExer Technologies. RangeForce, which is based in New York but whose technical teams are in Tallinn, is another Estonian company that is very active in the training of private companies, especially their developers and security experts.

Once again, there's a link in Estonia between public legal thinking and economic investment in a new sector. The country is positioning itself on subjects of the future: genetics and predictive medicine, artificial intelligence and robotics, cyber security and cyber hygiene. Its method is unique: solid political willingness, a quickly adaptable regulatory framework and an economic structure that features top-performing start ups and globally recognised experts.

Estonia isn't done surprising us.

10. Is Gafam a predator of the State? (Gafam vs. Democracy)

The end of the Westphalian State

The currently accepted notion of the nation-State's sovereignty took root in the 17th century with the signing of the Peace of Westphalia (1648), which put an end to the Thirty Years' War in Europe. This series of peace treaties protected the principle of sovereignty over geographic territory. Today however, this notion of the nation-State has been attacked on multiple fronts and jeopardised by the development of the digital economy. The next great disruption will have a huge effect on States, which will need to quickly adapt and evolve, if they want to persevere in the face of the digital giants that are expanding their domination and challenging the very notion of State sovereignty.

Taavi Kotka, former CEO of Nortal and former CIO of the Estonian government spoke on the urgency of this issue in a conference whose title was inspired by the TV series *Game of Thrones*: Winter is Coming!

During his presentation[1], he explained that changes in the music, taxi and hospitality industries (among others) will also affect public sectors. "We mustn't believe that States can escape that fate. Thinking that citizens will keep buying old services wherever they live is so 20th century!"

Tom Symons, a member of the think tank Nesta[2], chimed in with a similar message: "Platforms like Amazon are gearing up to replace entire government functions. If governments don't grasp the nettle, they may find themselves left behind by technology and other countries, which won't wait around for them."

Taavi Kotka quoted Albert Einstein as he urged political leaders to think differently about this challenge: "We cannot solve our problems with the same thinking we used when we created them."

In an exclusive interview with Dominique Nora[3], President Kersti Kaljulaid responded in the following terms to a question about whether the sovereignty of European States could be threatened by the powerful American digital platforms (GAFAM), which dominate the new global economy of data: "We cannot reproach these companies for offering digital solutions if public authorities aren't doing it! States have the duty to provide an identity to each citizen: we call that a passport. However, the digital is already everywhere... If governments don't give their citizens a sure way of verifying their identities online, they

1.   DLD Europe 17.

2.   The nation state goes virtual : why citizenship need no longer be determined by geography. *The New Statesman*, February 1, 2018.

3.   « Estonie : Bienvenue au e-Paradis » [Estonia: Welcome to e-Paradise], Dominique Nora, *L'Obs*, September 29, 2017.

will use the alternative services offered by Google or Microsoft. Without digital transformation, States will become obsolete."

The Estonian president sheds light on the tendency toward solutionism[4], meaning GAFAM's ability to bring better solutions than States, while removing the political or the democratic from these "solutions". This can start very simply: in Estonia, the digital training of the entire population was organised by the government. In France, Google opened its first digital workshop in Rennes at the start of June 2018, a decision that conforms to the idea that "the approach of the government is to accelerate digital transformation and thus to train as many people as possible".[5]But is every person who gives training neutral? Does GAFAM not have its own political objectives?

For the Belgian researcher Laurent Calixte, GAFAM is in fact a political party, in the sense that it's bound to take power and transform the world and human relationships.[6] This should make us think more about the contracts administrations sign with GAFAM. Etienne Gonnu refers to this in *Numérama*[7], where he wrote about the 2009 "open bar" contract between the French Ministry of Defence and Microsoft. This contract, signed without a call for bids or public

---

4.   A term coined by Evgeny Morozov in his book *To Save Everything, Click Here: The Folly of Technological Solutionism*, Public Affairs, 2014.

5.   *Ouest France*, June 8, 2018.

6.   Apple Google Amazon Facebook sont-ils devenu des partis politiques *Medium* August 30, 2016.

7.   « Contrat open bar de l'armée : la France doit entamer sa cure de désintoxication avec Microsoft ». *Numérama October 20 2017*

procedure and against the opinion of military experts, was renewed in 2013, and again in 2017...

The technological revolution redesigns the needs of citizens, the economy and borders

The technological revolution is clearing the way for new demands from citizens. As the world gradually changes, the public is getting familiar with new ways of doing things that are easier, online services, being able to instantly purchase things without leaving home, etc. They're expecting government and the civil service to use the same basics to simplify and facilitate access to their services. "I just think that most people already find that their governments are too far away. Their national governments are far away, Brussels is far away. The tendency is to go in the opposite direction—people want to have some kind of control over their lives. To vote for governments they can understand, where the rules are set, and they expect technology to adapt to these rules," explains Jakob von Uexküll, writer, activist and founder of the World Future Council.[8]

---

8. Where Stuff Happens First: White Paper on Estonia's Digital Ideology, Daniel Vaarik, *BDA*, think tank of the President of Estonia.

The technological revolution, by letting people work remotely, is opening up another destabilising front for State sovereignty

The significant changes in the economy that have come out of the technological revolution are also challenging the traditional social model and leading to a deep shift in the structure of labour. It is now possible to work from anywhere in the world, without being part of a single company or to work for different companies operating in different countries, all in one day. This disruption poses fundamental questions about consenting to pay taxes for public services that are being consumed elsewhere.

The decision to put up for a vote whether or not to maintain licence fees in Switzerland came out of the argument that one isn't necessarily obligated to pay for public television when one can have Netflix for less. Even if in this example, Télévision Suisse Romande won the day, we can see how some people might think that the public nature of a service is no longer enough to keep it, when compared to the simple question of quality of service. With this new attitude, there also arise new threats to the financial survival of the State.

The Estonian counter-model of the transnational State

Within the e-Residency programme, Taavi Kotka explains: "The marketplace for people who sell their brainpower represents $20 trillion. This is also the amount for the marketplace of people who can sell their services remotely, independent of their living space. And if they're in a position to sell their services anywhere in the world, they're going to spend most of their money in their place of residence..."[9]

President Kersti Kaljulaid adds, "We recognise that there is the need to think about tax systems if people work in five different companies, in five different countries, at the same time. This needs to be sorted out. We cannot sort it alone, we need to sort it out globally."[10]

"In 2018, citizenship will no longer be determined by the geographic borders of a country," says Tom Symons, a member of the Nesta think tank. For the American venture capitalist, Ben Horowitz, the classic State is already gone: "Network is the Leviathan, as opposed to the State. The new State would be a network, not a geography. When you have a potential to opt into the country that you want to be part of, as opposed to it being the function of where you live, you are a citizen of this network."[11] 25 years after Robert Reich and his concept of the enterprise network, it's now public structures that are on the receiving end of the blowout, with the small difference that the citizens themselves are creating their own State-networks.

9.   DLD Europe 17.

10. "From AI to Russia, here's how Estonia's President is planning for the future", *Wired*, April 5, 2018.

11. *Where Stuff Happens First: White Paper on Estonia's Digital Ideology*, Daniel Vaarik, BDA, think tank of the President of Estonia.

The virtual nation is coming

In a 2017 article for the think tank Nesta called, "The nation state goes virtual", Tom Symons describes the arrival of the virtual nation: "There are movements taking advantage of decentralising technologies, in a bid to do away with the nation state altogether. In this category, the example of Bitnation is a compelling one. Bitnation is a blockchain-based technology enabling people to create and join virtual nations. This allows people to agree to their own social contracts between one another, using smart contract technology, removing the need for governments as administrators or mediators. Since it began in 2014, Bitnation has been offering traditional government services, such as notaries, dispute resolution, marriages and voting systems, without the need for a middleman.

As of November 2017, there are over 10,000 Bitnation citizens. Bitnation believes its model can have a huge impact in the developing world, where restrictions citizens face on incorporating businesses or protecting property rights, for example, are far greater than in western democracies. Bitnation is positioning itself to meet this demand in the developing world and believes that being taken up in emerging markets will put pressure on mature markets, which will need to adapt the same governance speed and flexibility to remain competitive."

This, more broadly, is the model advocated by a few billionaire libertarians, who wish to free themselves from the State, like Peter Thiel, one of the founders of PayPal, who finances the project from floating cities in international waters.

Faced with these phenomena, Estonia must now consider questions that go far beyond e-Government and are concerned with the idea of citizenship and the State of tomorrow.

The Estonian response: change the concept of citizenship

The online identification system is an attempt to "redefine the nature of the country" by getting rid of bureaucracy and reinventing Government as a Service. Andres Kütt, Chief Architect of the Estonian Information System Authority, confirms this.

For Kütt, a young graduate of MIT and former employee of Skype, this idea of "Government as a Service" aims to integrate each person's data into one, easy-to-navigate portal. "Estonia wants to smash bureaucratic silos and distribute power down to the citizens, so that the government comes to them, rather than their having to go to the government. We are changing the concept of citizenship. This technology creates trust. It's transparent. All agencies can access this data, but citizens have the right to know if their data has been accessed. In the old world, citizens were dependent on government; in Estonia, we are trying to make government dependent on citizens."[12]

"In a way (in e-Estonia), the government and the public sector are serving you and you're in the driver's seat: you have control. Or at least, more so

12. "Where in the world will you find the most advanced e-Government? Estonia",ideas.ted.com, March 15, 2018.

than in other societies. The citizen is a subject, and not an object of government. That change of philosophy, I think that you are the only country where this is being implemented," confirms Mikko Kosonen, the director of the Finland think tank SITRA.[13]

Country as a Service: Estonia pioneers the reinvented State as service provider

In response to all these disruptive factors, certain governments are using these changes as an occasion to reconceptualise what we think of when we hear the word "nation-State". Faced with the solutionism of GAFAM, States must bring solutions to citizens that are just as effective, but which also guarantee their fundamental rights and respect for their political will.

By creating the e-Residency solution in 2014, Estonia gave access to its public services and economy to citizens across the globe by allowing them to create companies remotely. Estonia, in excusing e-Residents of their physical presence in the country, is paving the way for a new model of the virtual nation-State within which, citizenship will no longer be determined by geography.

As Kaspar Korjus, former Estonian e-Residency Programme Director, explains, "In Estonia, we believe that people should be able to freely choose the public digital services that best fit them, regardless of the geographical area where they were arbitrarily born...

---

13. *Where Stuff Happens First: White Paper on Estonia's Digital Ideology*, Daniel Vaarik, BDA, think tank of the President of Estonia.

We're truly living in exciting times when nation States and virtual States compete and collaborate with each other on an international market to provide better governance services."[14] "Estonia is the first Nation without borders, which looks past its borders into the digital universe," declares Kaspar Korjus. For Jean-Michel Billaut, founder of L'Atelier BNP Paribas, "Estonians are well on their way to creating a supra-nationality."

According to Kaspar Korjus[15], "It's a problem for a country if the digital wave isn't well directed. For now, this is only a matter of improving the administrative mechanism (and the economic one, as a result) but, in ten years, it's the fundamental question of the State's income that will be impacted. In ten years, the world will be in a position to freely choose to belong to a digital nation, and people will not choose the country whose administration is the most demanding and which depends, simultaneously, on paperwork and people. Just like in Italy and in England, France must really start doing this. Estonia is ready to help other countries in their steps."[16]

For Arnaud Castaignet[17], "e-Residency opens up new perspectives: what services are you going to use in your own country if you're a digital citizen in ten other countries? What will the revenue sources for States be if cryptocurrency is developed?"

14. *NS tech*, Tom Symons, February 1, 2018.

15. Former Estonian e-Residency Programme Director, now co-founder at Pactum.

16. Interview with the authors, used in the *Meunier Qui Dort* blog, June 2017.

17. Former Head of Public Relations for the Estonian e-Residency programme.

These are the questions that Estonia is asking itself.

For *Institut Sapiens*: "the establishment of new public programmes aims to prolong the State as a platform by disassociating it more and more from a territory: digital sovereignty, the research into and establishment of regulatory frameworks adapted to new technologies and economic models" are part of the brand for this new kind of State as a platform, which "offers to create a State without borders that has authority over a 'digital nation'."[18] Estonia is inviting us to redefine the meaning of a nation-State in the digital age. As we move from the idea of Government as a Platform to that of "Country as a Service", and anticipate that seamless services will be the next step, the question is: will the 21st century State need to be invisible in order to survive?

What are the implications of these changes for States?

Now is the time for governments to start taking all the implications of the digital age seriously. From electronic identification and data management to transparent access to services, citizens will continue asking for digital services of the highest quality. Three countries (Azerbaijan, Lithuania and Kazakhstan) have already declared themselves in favour of developing

---

18. « L'e-Estonie, modèle d'un état plateforme e-gouverné », Institut Sapiens, July 2018.

e-Residency programmes. The entry of the Estonian government into the data sector is leading the way to new potentials, all with extremely significant results. This could result in a new rivalry between sovereign governments and the private superpowers of Silicon Valley. "Governments are realising that they're losing the digital identities of their citizens to American companies like Google, Facebook, Amazon and Apple. And they are waking up to the realisation that they have a responsibility to protect the privacy of these citizens," says Linnar Viik, Director of the e-Governance Academy.[19]

For the researcher, Kadi Maria Vooglaid, "the next chapter for Estonia doesn't need to be yet another glitzy e-something project. What the global community needs is governments that understand the moral consequences of the impact of technologies on people's lives and the capacity to regulate that new reality. Estonia, as the pioneer of e-Government, should take the lead in this global conversation."[20]

This democratic issue was underlined during the Latitude59 conference in May 2018 in Tallinn. Today, it's often missing from discussions about technology, artificial intelligence and the point of singularity[21], a topic that transcends the competition between States and GAFAM, since it will touch at the very nature of humanity.

---

19. "Where in the world will you find the most advanced e-Government? Estonia", ideas.ted.com, March 15, 2018.

20. "What should be the state's role in a digital future?",*Estonian World*, January 10, 2018.

21. The moment when technologies like AI will achieve a level where humanity will no longer be able to follow them.

The potential implications of virtual residences are enormous and could result in governments that are radically different from those of today. The digital revolution will allow access to a greater number of online services, from anywhere in the world. Today, the advantages of e-Residency lie in doing business in another jurisdiction, but in the future, the services provided could expand to the supplying of currencies, education and health services.

As citizens, we will be in a position to educate our children in Finland, access health care in South Korea and manage our companies in New Zealand, without having to leave the comfort of our homes. Governments might see in this model a way to achieve long-term financial viability: generating income by selling services to a global population instead of centralised taxation systems that involve a single geographic population.

Neelie Kroes, European Commission for the Digital Agenda (2010-2014), stated, "So, the idea of national borders and systems, the old idea of fixed equipment, these things will become less and less relevant..."[22] Certain States are preparing themselves for this new reality by highlighting their services, also available for non-nationals, in a new form of transnational citizenship.

The "Country as a Service" model refers to a system in which countries will offer different levels of citizenship and will tax citizens based on the number of services they've used and the citizenship level

---

22. *Where Stuff Happens First: White Paper on Estonia's Digital Ideology*, Daniel Vaarik, BDA, think tank of the President of Estonia.

they've chosen. This would mean having multiple kinds of citizenships, including city-States and virtual nations.

Behind this redefining of what the nation-State is at this time of digital revolution, there's also the issue of what the European vision of the digital is: meaning, the establishment of a European model of the modern State, which would take into account and adapt to changes, in order to ensure its own longevity. "Unless we can fix the current democratic system, we will not have a chance. Because all the problems we are facing now in Europe and in Finland with structural changes are almost impossible to carry out with the current democratic structure and governance models. They are too short-sighted and rigid," explains Mikko Kosonen, director of the think tank SITRA.[23]

It's the State itself which is on the brink of disappearing, unless it starts taking on its own digital transformation. Whole sections of public services could be wiped out and replaced with GAFAM's easy-to-use applications. A movement which can be incorporated into public transformation within the framework of civic tech. "Estonia is the European alternative to the Silicon Valley model. A digital society centred on the citizen and built on trust. This country embraces the future, by guarding its social values and its sense of community—in perfect accord with Jeremy Rifkin's shared collective", insists Kevin Chavanne, Partnership Coordinator at Funderbeam.

---

23. *Where Stuff Happens First: White Paper on Estonia's Digital Ideology*, Daniel Vaarik, BDA, think tank of the President of Estonia.

The "full digital" Estonia, extending across the European scale, would be an effective shield against the increasingly invasive interference of American GAFAM and Chinese BATX (referring to Chinese tech giants Baidu, Alibaba, Tencent and Xiaomi). As French senator Bruno Retailleau[24] put it, "we shouldn't have to choose between being a digital colony to the United States or China!" And that reality is much closer than we might think. Michel Paulin, CEO of OVHcloud, one of the largest hosting providers in Europe, recently declared[25]: "French ministers don't know that their data is being hosted on American servers". The creation of a public European cloud, which Estonia recommended during its presidency of the EU Council, has become an urgent need.

This would be a truly effective alliance, one that confronts issues surrounding the economy, citizenship and the meaning of public service. We weren't mistaken: we are very much seeing the clash of two models. Woe unto those democracies which haven't grasped the urgency of how their State is transforming. The Cambridge Analytica scandal exposed GAFAM's true impact on our democracies, which compelled Facebook to react. States also tried to react, including France with its law on fake news. However, for their efforts to be effective, they would have needed to establish a kind of co-regulation with the

---

24. Bruno Retailleau, Edouard Fillias, « Devenir une colonie numérique américaine voire chinoise ? Nous devons refuser cette fatalité » [Become a digital colony to America or China? We must refuse this fate], *L'Opinion*, November 5, 2019.

25. Interview with francetvinfo.fr on November 9, 2019.

tech giants, a relationship that is entirely up to the latter's discretion.

When we published the French edition of this book, we were invited to numerous conferences, including one at the Ministry of Economy and Finance and another at the Court of Auditors. The Estonian model interested the attendees, but there was always the same scepticism when confronted with the question of how to compete against GAFAM. In our arguments, we always used the example of healthcare, an area where GAFAM has made great advances, but this was before Facebook announced its plans to create Libra. Today, there is no doubt that the ever-growing threat against sovereign prerogative will directly lead to States finally reacting and showing interest in what this small Baltic State has to offer!

Let's not forget that our freedom lies at the heart of this subject; sovereign prerogatives ensure that our societies can democratically function. By attacking them, GAFAM endangers what the rule of law guarantees us and by applying the decisions and predictions of AI to daily life, GAFAM controls every person's free will. There are two battles for freedom playing out behind the issue of the potential obsolescence of States in the digital age: the freedom of citizens and the freedom of individuals to make decisions by themselves. In this sense, the questions of data ownership and storage are crucial: that is, if we'd like to prevent our data from being used to feed quantum computers that help enrich a few stakeholders, to the detriment of our choices about society, life and what we consume. The *Financial Times* recently ran a fantastic article on this important subject, entitled: "Our personal data needs protecting from Big Tech.".[26]

The digital revolution will continue changing the codes and the fundamentals of power. At a time when students in a garage are capable of standing up to whole sections of the global economy, a small country galvanised by its youth and need to survive could be in a position to lead Europe onto the path of a new digital model that might save the future of democracy.

Will Estonia enter history as the first model of the nation-State in the digital age? We have no doubt that in the future, the Estonian model will be taught in school, right next to the classic political models. Nevertheless, Estonia's 30-year-experience clearly demonstrates that the digital age is more about mind-set than anything else and that technology is not the solution, but rather, a tool in the service of a vision. As such, the "Estonian Way" should be seen as a leading example of how to maintain human-centric States during the digital age.

Breaking the walls

30 years after the fall of the Berlin Wall and the resurgence of European liberty as an ideal, let's not forget that our freedom isn't only a matter of the physical, but also the political, including in the digital sphere. This is the lesson we can learn from Estonia: being a "full digital" State means inventing the digital

---

26. The *Financial Times*, November 17, 2019.

sovereignty of the State and its citizens in the face of all-powerful transnational actors. It's a new crack in the wall.

Ressources

3 Gilles Babinet: "There is a shift in sovereignty from States to GAFA." *France Inter*, August 14, 2018.

4 Extract from the brochure *Estonia Oh Surprise!*, published by the Estonian Ministry of Foreign Affairs.

10 *Indépendant*, April 27, 2013, "Carcassonne officiellement unie à Tallinn sa sœur du Nord".

11 Jean-Pierre Minaudier, *Histoire de l'Estonie et de la nation estonienne* [History of Estonia and the Estonian Nation], L'Harmattan, 2007.

14 « Comment les États baltes ont-ils réclamé leur indépendance grâce à une chaîne humaine record ? » [How did the Baltic States reclaim their independence with a record-breaking human chain?] Boris Egorov, fr.rbth.com, August 15, 2018.

16 Lauri Vahtre, *Estonians Inside Out*, Pilgrim, 2017.

18 "Is This Tiny European Nation a Preview of Our Tech Future?", *Fortune*, April 27, 2017.

19 France – Pays baltes. La force d'une relation trop lointaine [France – Baltic Countries. The Strength of a Very Remote Relationship], *Félix Torres* Éditeur, 2010.

22 "Estonie, se reconstruire par le numérique"[Estonia: Rebuilding Itself Through Digital Technology], *Renaissance numérique*, 2015.

23 Jeremy Rifkin, The End of Work: The Decline of the Global Labor Force and the Dawn of the Post-Market Era, *Putnam Publishing Group*, 1995.

24 "How tiny Estonia stepped out of old USSR's shadow to become an internet titan", *The Guardian*, 2012.

25 The Heritage Foundation.

28 Creating a digital society: Can Australia learn something from Estonia?" *cio.com*, February 17, 2018.

29 "Estonia the Digital Republic", *The New Yorker*, December 18, 2017.

30 "Bienvenue en e-Estonia" [Welcome to e-Estonia], *Les Échos*, December 1, 2014.

33 Government as a platform, Marggetts&Naumann, 2016.

36 "I'm former Estonian president Toomas Hendrik Ilves, and This is How I Work", *Lifehacker*, October 16, 2019.

37 "How tiny Estonia stepped out of USSR's shadow to become an internet titan", *The Guardian*, 2012.

38 "Estonia, the Skype effect", *BBC News*, May 13, 2016.

41 "Where in the world will you find the most advanced e-government? Estonia", ideas.ted.com, March 15, 2018.

45 Estonian Government, *Life in Estonia*, February 2018.

48 "Building the Digital Government – Estonia's Digital Transformation", Under the Hood, October 26, 2019.

50 L'e-Estonie, modèle d'un État plateforme e-gouverné [E-Estonia, model of an e-governed platform-state], *Institut Sapiens*, July 2018.

56 "*How Estonia nurtures a national digital identity*", Global Intelligence for the CIO, August 2019.

57 *e-Estonia: e-Governance in Practice*, e-Governance Academy, 2017

58 "There is no blockchain technology in the X-Road", *NIIS*, April 26, 2018.

60 "Estonia ready to share e-state experience with world", *The baltic course*, May 10, 2018.

63 Bienvenue en e-Estonie, le premier État réel à l'administration 100% dématérialisée" [Welcome to e-Estonia, the First Real State with a 100% Digital Administration]. *L'Opinion*, June 5, 2017.

65 "How Estonia nurtures a national digital identity", *Global intelligence for the CIO*, August 2019.

69 "Learning from the Estonian e-health system", *Health Europa*, January 2019.

71 "Building the Digital Government – Estonia's Digital Transformation", *Under the Hood*, October 26, 2019.

72 "Estonia experiments with blockchain, smart services and 'data embassies'", *GCN*, April 4, 2018.

74 "Creating a digital society: Can Australia learn something from Estonia?", *cio.com*, February 17, 2018.

75 "Estonie : Bienvenue au e-Paradis" [Estonia: Welcome to e-Paradise], Dominique Nora, *L'Obs*, September 29, 2017.

76 E-stonia: the country using tech to rebrand itself as the anti-Russia", *The Guardian*, April 21, 2016.

79 « Monaco l'autre Estonie du Luxembourg » [Monaco, the other Estonia in Luxembourg], *Paperjam*, May 10, 2019.

80 "Cyber threats no longer know national borders", *e-estonia*, September 2019.

83 *Government as a platform*, Marggetts&Naumann.

89 "What Are The Biggest Industries In Estonia?",*World Atlas*, July 2, 2019.

90 *Life in Estonia*, March, 2016.

92, 95 "How Tallinn's tech talent transformed its start-up ecosystem on Thursday", *elite business*, January 18, 2018.

96 « Bienvenue en Estonie » [Welcome to Estonia], *Enjeux les Echos*, October 12, 2014. The title of Entrepreneur of the Year in Estonia was given by the firm EY Estonia.

97 "How Estonia has avoided EU's economic problems", Charlotte Ashton, *BBC news*, October 6, 2011.

100 "The Skype Effect", *BBC News*, May 13, 2016.

101 *Hacker news*, May 2016.

103 "Estonian mafia looking for the next generation of entrepreneurs", Cyrus Farivar, *ArsTechnica*, November 6, 2012

106 "10 Estonian startups to look out for in 2019 and beyond", *EU-Startups*, Janurary 11, 2019.

107 "Chasing Unicorns: A hilarious new movie about Estonian entrepreneurs taking on the world", Adam Rang. *Estonian World*, September 14, 2019.

110 "How did Estonia become a leader in technology? By ditching legacy technology and betting on education", *The Economist*, July 31, 2013.

111 "Tech-savvy Estonia wants you to know it has 1.3m people — and 4 unicorns", *The Hustle*, July 5, 2018.

112 "A small country has only one natural resource – between our ears", Kersti Kaljulaid, *Estonian world*, February 24, 2017, published in 2018.

113, 114 "L'Estonie, le pays des 'e-citoyens'" [Estonia, the country of 'e-citizens'], *Les Echos*, February 10, 2016.

117 "L'entrepreneur sans frontière" [The entrepreneur without borders] on the blog *Le Meunier Qui Dort*, May 2017.

119 "Why Estonia succeeds at public innovation", *US News* (Best countries rankings), February 8, 2018.

120 "Devenir e-Resident : comment la nationalité numérique fait rayonner l'Estonie" [Becoming an e-Resident: how digital nationality makes Estonia shine], *Mashable*, October 4, 2017.

121 e-resident.gov.ee.

122 "Who are Estonia's e-Residents? Estonia became the first country to offer e-Residency 3 years ago & now has nearly 30,000 people from 139 countries signed up", Adam Rang, *Medium*, November 30, 2017.

123 "British entrepreneur Vicky Brock is using e-Residency to protect consumers from online crime", Adam Rang.

124 "There's an app for that, Our new community network will give e-Residents more opportunities to connect, learn and grow companies, E-Residency", *Medium*.

126 "How Tallinn's tech talent transformed its startup ecosystem on Thursday", *elitebusiness*, January 18, 2018.

127 "Estonia's E-Residency Contributed €14M To Its Economy--' E-Residency 2.0 Will Be A True Forerunner'", *Forbes*, April 25, 2019.

131 "Why Estonia pioneered digital identity", *TechRadar,* September 3, 2019.

134 "Estonia declared the best country for digital life", *Estonian World*, May 30, 2019.

138 "What should be the state's role in a digital future?", *Estonian world*, January 2018.

139 *Life in Estonia*, February 2018.

140 *e-estonia*.

141 *MIT Press Journal*, July 18, 2011.

142 2017 Oxford University research paper.

144 « L'e-administration, un objectif plus facile à dire qu'à atteindre » [E-Administration, easier said than done], *earchimag.com*, February 7, 2018.

147 Fondapol.org

150 The true start-up nation *Society*, April 19, 2018.

152 After Europe, Ivan Krastev, *Penn University Press*, 2017.

156 "President Kersti Kaljulaid participated in the 29th Étape du Tour de France on Sunday July 21, 2019 ERR.ee, July 22, 2019.

158 *Madame Figaro*, January 14, 2018.

163 "A small country has only one natural resource – between our ears", Kersti Kaljulaid, *Estonian World*, February 24, 2017, published in 2018.

164 "Estonia is one of the most homophobic countries in the OECD", *Estonian world*, May 2018.

165 "European human rights authority: Estonia needs more social cohesion", *Estonian world*, June 2018.

169 "Over 30 Estonian tech companies sign a green pledge to become climate neutral", *Estonian World*, September 17, 2019.

171 President Kersti Kajulaid, "Il faut parler avec la Russie, mais sans naïveté" [We must talk to Russia, but we mustn't be naive about it], *France 24*, November 18, 2019.

172 "The era of Trump means it is time for small States to start thinking big", *Euronews*, July 2, 2018.

176 Bilan numérique de la présidence estonienne [Digital assessment of the Estonian presidency], Clément Harmegnies, *Le Taurillon*, February 16, 2018.

181 The Baltic States Turn 100. One lesson we have learned is that the benefits of freedom can be wide-ranging and unpredictable. *The Wall Street Journal*, February 7, 2018.

185 Connectedhealth.ee, July 2017.

187, 192 "Estonia Wants to Collect the DNA of All Its Citizens", *The Atlantic*, October 8, 2015.

191 news.err.ee, March 2018.

196 *La Tribune*, June 8, 2018.

201 "Building the Digital Government – Estonia's Digital Transformation", *Under the Hood*, October 26, 2019.

202 "Estonia: From AI judges to robot bartenders, is the post-Soviet state the dark horse of digital tech?" *ABC*.

205 From AI to Russia, Here's How Estonia's President Is Planning for the Future *Wired*, April 5, 2018.

206 *212 DLD Europe 17.*

207 The nation state goes virtual : why citizenship need no longer be determined by geography. *The New Statesman*, February 1, 2018.

208 « Estonie : Bienvenue au e-Paradis » [Estonia: Welcome to e-Paradise], Dominique Nora, *L'Obs*, September 29.

209 A term coined by Evgeny Morozov in his book *To Save Everything, Click Here: The Folly of Technological Solutionism*, Public Affairs, 2014.

210 *Ouest France*, June 8, 2018.

211 Apple Google Amazon Facebook sont-ils devenu des partis politiques ? *Medium* August 30, 2016.

212 « Contrat open bar de l'armée : la France doit entamer sa cure de désintoxication avec Microsoft ». *Numérama*, October 20, 2017.

213, 216 *Where Stuff Happens First: White Paper on Estonia's Digital Ideology*, Daniel Vaarik, BDA.

215 "From AI to Russia, here's how Estonia's President is planning for the future", *Wired*, April 5, 2018.

217 "Where in the world will you find the most advanced e-Government? Estonia",ideas.ted.com, March 15, 2018.

223 « L'e Estonie, modèle d'un état plateforme e-gouverné », Institut Sapiens, July 2018.

225 "What should be the state's role in a digital future?", *Estonian World*, January 10, 2018.

229 Bruno Retailleau, Edouard Fillias, « Devenir une colonie numérique américaine voire chinoise ? Nous devons refuser cette fatalité » [Become a digital colony to America or China? We must refuse this fate], *L'Opinion*, November 5, 2019.

230 Interview with francetvinfo.fr on November 9, 2019.

231 Our personal data needs protecting from Big Tech The *Financial Times*, November 17, 2019.

CONTENTS TABLE

ACKNOWLEDGEMENTS

We'd like to express our most sincere thanks to:

Our contacts, for sharing their knowledge and expertise with us:

Geoffroy Berson, former Attaché for Cooperation on Digital Innovation at the French Institute of Estonia in Tallinn

Jean-Michel Billaut, founder of L'Atelier BNP Paribas

Henri Capoul, General Manager of Bolt in France

Arnaud Castaignet, former Head of Public Relations for the e-Residency programme

Kevin Chavanne, Partnership Coordinator at Funderbeam

Chantal de Bourmont, President of the France-Estonia Association

Romain de La Ville, former Project Manager of the Bolloré Group

Dominique Dubarry, author of the book, *France-Pays baltes, la force d'une relation trop lointaine* [France and the Baltic countries: the power of a very distant relationship]

Pierre Gronlier, former employee at Skype in Tallinn

Klen Jäärats, Director for European Union Affairs in the State Chancellery

Dmitri Jegorov, Undersecretary for Tax and Customs Policy at the Estonian Ministry of Finance

Marten Kaevats, National Digital Advisor of the Estonian government

Siim Kallas, former Prime Minster and EU Commissioner

Kaspar Korjus, former Managing Director of the e-Residency programme

Andres Kütt, Chief Architect of the Estonian Information System Authority

Kadi Metsandi, Director of Development Cooperation and Humanitarian Aid at the Estonian Foreign Ministry

Paul Regnard, former participant in the international trainee programme VIE (*Volontariat International en Entreprises*) in Estonia

Xavier Schneider, pharmacist and entrepreneur

Siim Sikkut, Estonian government Chief Information Officer

Our attentive readers for their astute guidance:

Carole Barjon, editorial writer at *L'Obs*

Geoffroy Berson, former Attaché for Cooperation on Digital Innovation at the French Institute of Estonia in Tallinn

Volker Klostius, musicologist and holder of an *agrégation* (a high-level competitive exam in France) in German

Jérôme Wallut, partner at ICP Consulting

The invaluable people we met along the way:

H.E. Clyde Kull, Estonian Ambassador to France

H.E. Alar Streimann, former Estonian Ambassador to France

H.E. Éric Lamouroux, French Ambassador to Estonia

H.E. Claudia Delmas-Scherer, former French Ambassador to Estonia

Ain Aaviksoo, former Under Secretary for e-Services and Innovation in Healthcare

Kristel Amelie Aimre, Economic and Trade Attaché at the Estonian Embassy in Paris

Aymeric Bourdin, President of the think tank Atelier Europe

Philippe Cadic, doctor and engineer

Hélène Campourcy, President of the association Pink Innov'

Jean Capelli, start upper

Mads Emil Dalsgaard, former Chief Marketing Officer at Funderbeam

Patrick d'Humières, Director of the Académie Durable Internationale

Didier de Thoisy, Social Network Community Manager

Jean-Michel Enard, Vice-President of the Franco-Estonian Chamber of Commerce

Capucine Fandre, President of Séance Publique

Matthieu Fouquet, Secretary General of Onepoint

Anders Hedman, President of the Franco-Estonian Chamber of Commerce

Jérôme Jubelin, founder of Umanao

Kristiina Kalda, Export Advisor for Enterprise Estonia

Tarmo Kiivit, international and public sector expert at Helmes

Tobias Koch, Business Engagement Manager for e-Estonia

David Layani, President of Onepoint

Sébastien Le Roux, Attaché for Digital Innovation at the French Institute of Estonia

Mari-Liis Lind, board member at Tech Sisters

Gregory Lu, co-founder of Natufia Labs

Pascal Millard, former Economic Counselor at the French Embassy in Estonia

Coryne Nicq, Communications Director

Anett Numa, speaker at the e-Estonia briefing centre

Indrek Õnnik, former Project Manager for e-Estonia

Thomas Padovani, Investor and founder at Adcash

Urmas Peiker, co-founder of Funderbeam

Carl Pucci, International Director of DatelOvela

Hector de Rivoire, Head of the Economic Department at the French Embassy in Estonia

Isa Schultz, member of the Board of Directors at the think tank Atelier Europe

Marek Tamm, Professor of Cultural History at Tallinn University

Anne Testuz, President of ATC Communications

Madis Tiik, doctor and public health expert

Nadim Taoubi COO at Natufia Labs

Special thanks to our translator, Nafkote Tamirat, and to everyone who inspired or encouraged this project.

ACHEVÉ D'IMPRIMER

Ce livre a été achevé d'imprimer pour le compte
de Cent Mille Milliards par Lightning Source,
1 avenue Gutenberg 78310 Maurepas.

Préparation et correction : Cent Mille Milliards.
Mise en page : Bärbel Müllbacher.

Typographies : à l'intérieur
Coline Première et Coline Cursive © Emilie Rigaud,
A is for Apple ; en couverture, Gotham © Hoefler & Co.

ISBN : 978-2-85071-013-1

Cent Mille Milliards
1014@centmillemilliards.com
www.centmillemilliards.com

Made in United States
North Haven, CT
08 May 2022

19018634R00143